DECORATIVE PAINTING TECHNIQUES BOOK

OVER 50 TECHNIQUES FOR CONVINCING BRUSHSTROKES AND PAINT EFFECTS

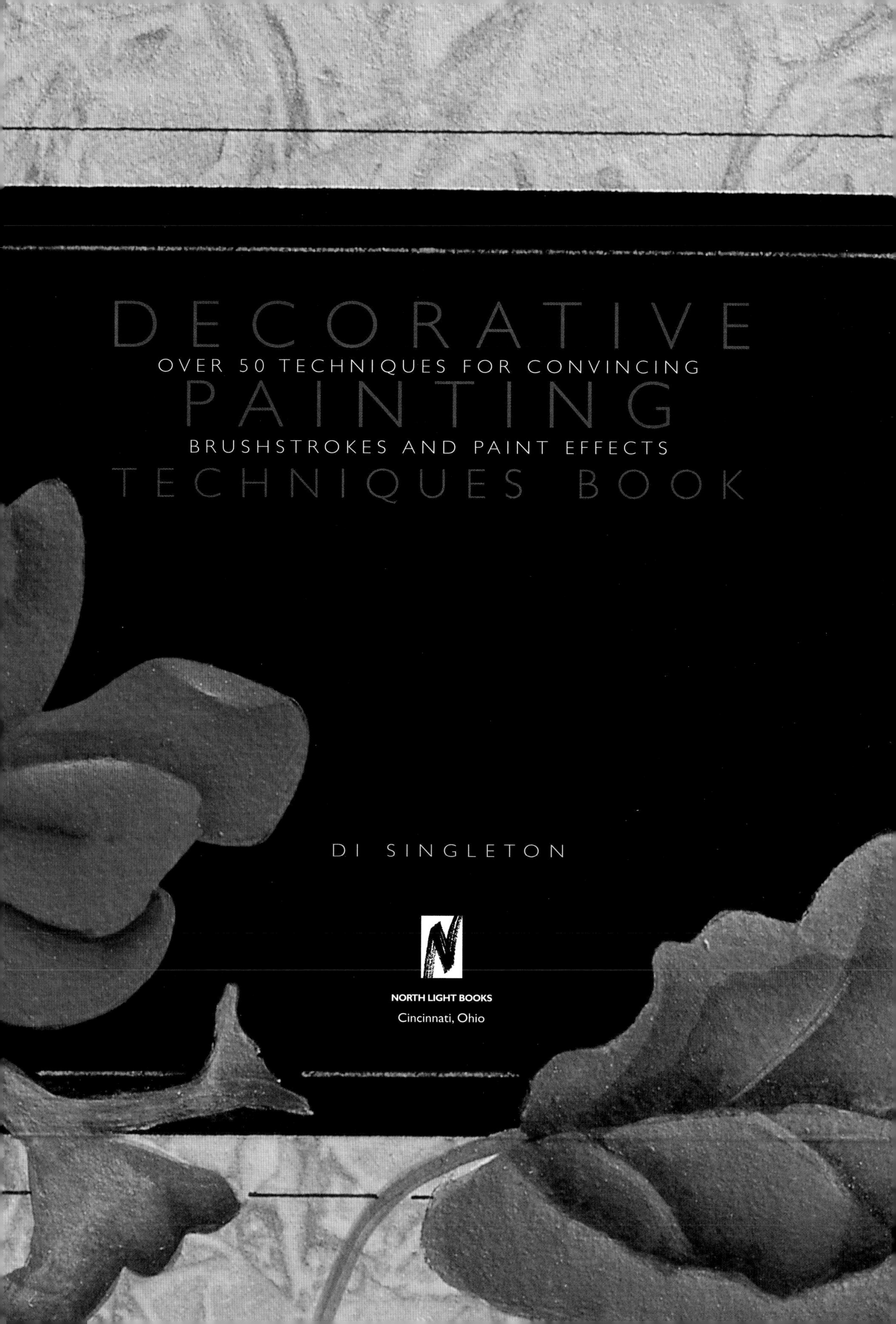

DECORATIVE PAINTING TECHNIQUES BOOK

OVER 50 TECHNIQUES FOR CONVINCING BRUSHSTROKES AND PAINT EFFECTS

DI SINGLETON

NORTH LIGHT BOOKS
Cincinnati, Ohio

A QUARTO BOOK

First published in North America in 2001 by
North Light Books, an imprint of F&W Publications, Inc.,
1507 Dana Avenue, Cincinnati,
OH 45207

ISBN 1-58180-252-8

QUAR.DWPT

Conceived, designed, and produced by
Quarto Publishing plc
The Old Brewery
6 Blundell Street
London N7 9BH

Project editor Marie-Claire Muir
Art editor Sheila Volpe
Designer Penny Dawes
Assistant art director Penny Cobb
Photographer Pat Aithie
Illustrator Tony Walter-Bellue
Copy editor Claire Waite
Proofreader Dierdre Clark
Indexer Dorothy Frame

Art director Moira Clinch
Publisher Piers Spence

Manufactured by
Universal Graphics PL
Singapore
Printed by Leefung-Asco
Printers Ltd, China

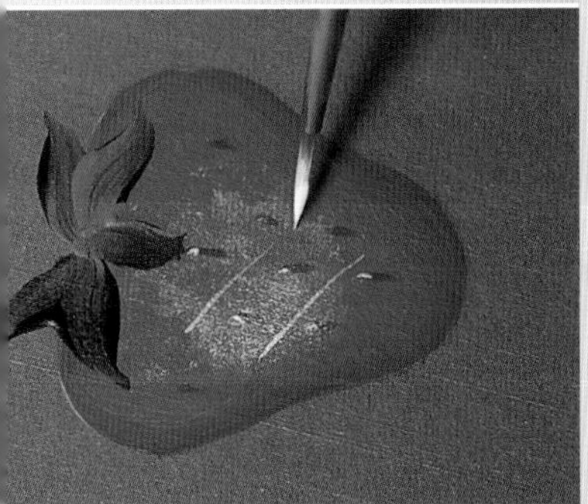
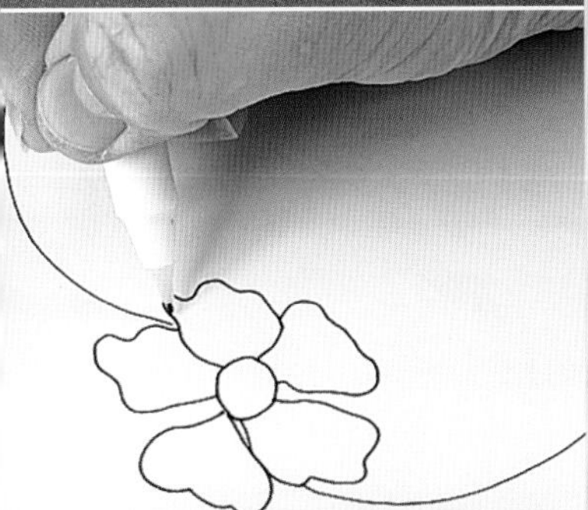

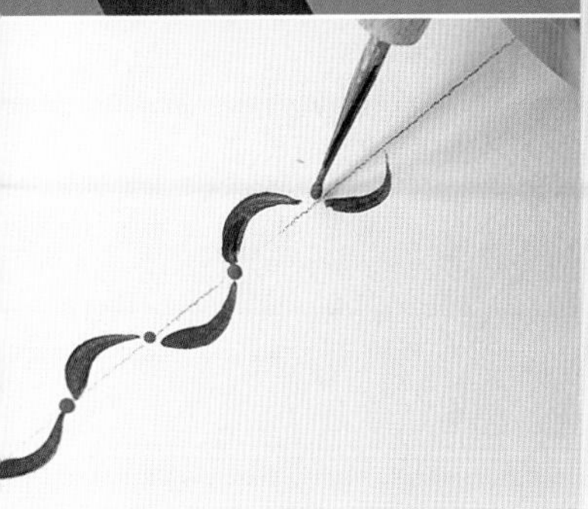

contents

CONTENTS

INTRODUCTION

PICK UP A BRUSH AND PAINT!

Decorative painting is a "learnable" art form. By taking a structured approach to the basic strokework, designs can be built up and then embellished more as more skills are acquired.

This book is particularly designed for people who have never painted before or who have painted in a different medium, but some of the techniques will also interest more experienced artists. "I can't paint," "I can't draw," and "I don't know how," will quickly change to "I can do," because the only thing difficult about decorative painting is believing that you can.

Unlike fine art, the starting point in decorative painting can be a preprepared design, rather than a dauntingly blank sheet of paper. Start decorative painting and you will find every magazine you pick up is full of ideas, even a line drawing

- ABOVE TOP
  Country and farmyard themes are popular subjects for decorative painters
- ABOVE
  A small bathroom cupboard, painted with intricate detail
- RIGHT
  A sumptuous floral design in Russian "Zhostovo" style

"THE ONLY THING DIFFICULT ABOUT PAINTING IS BELIEVING YOU CAN DO IT"

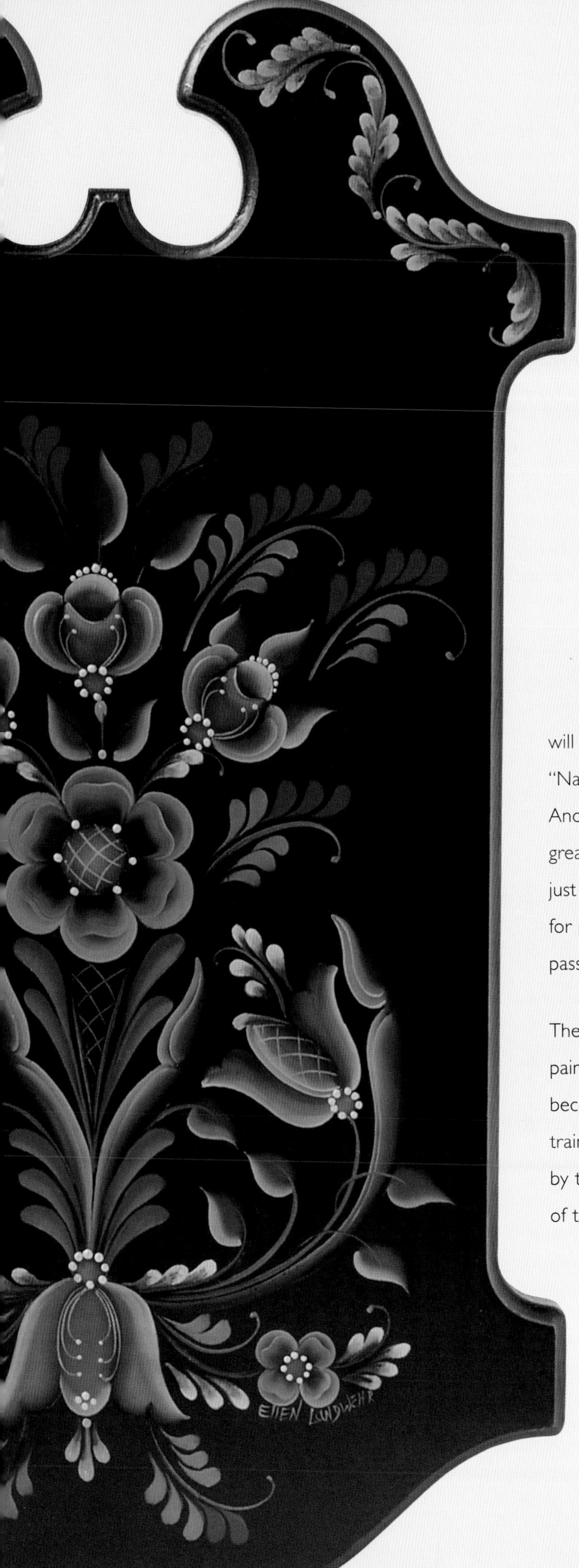

BELOW
Flowers and acorns decorate this polished wooden clockface

will get you thinking about how you would paint it. "Naked" wood will never have looked so interesting. Another bonus of decorative painting is that it's a great way to beat stress. When you are painting you just can't think of anything else, and it curbs the urge for retail therapy—though you may find that you can't pass a piece of bare wood without buying it.

The emphasis on techniques in this book aims to give painters a good grounding in the skills needed to become a competent artist. I have no formal art training, so most of my knowledge has been picked up by trial and error and from classes with a wide variety of teachers. I have learned something from every teacher I have had a class with, so if you are serious about learning to paint, take classes with as many teachers as possible. In this book I will try to pass on some of the knowledge I have gained to you.

ABOVE
The border and centerpiece on this serving tray work beautifully together; the grapes appear ready to burst with ripeness.

BELOW
A simple tin milk churn decorated with a pastoral scene and flora and fauna from the countryside.

The instructions take you through each technique with opportunities to practice and reinforce the skills you have learned in the form of mini projects. No one likes to do pages and pages of practice, so these little projects are a fun way to learn. The main projects then build on the techniques learned and take the painter step-by-step to fully finished pieces, with ideas for further experimentation and design.

There is nothing more satisfying than amazing yourself or your friends with a newly painted piece. If you are prepared to make the effort to practice and are willing to experiment, you can quickly become a competent decorative painter, even if you have never picked up a brush before.

The main thing to remember is to have fun and explore your creative side.

HAPPY PAINTING!

HOW TO USE THIS BOOK

Each chapter follows the same format: strokes and techniques are demonstrated, with small practice projects. At the end of each chapter, a large project enables you to follow through, step-by-step, to complete a whole finished piece.

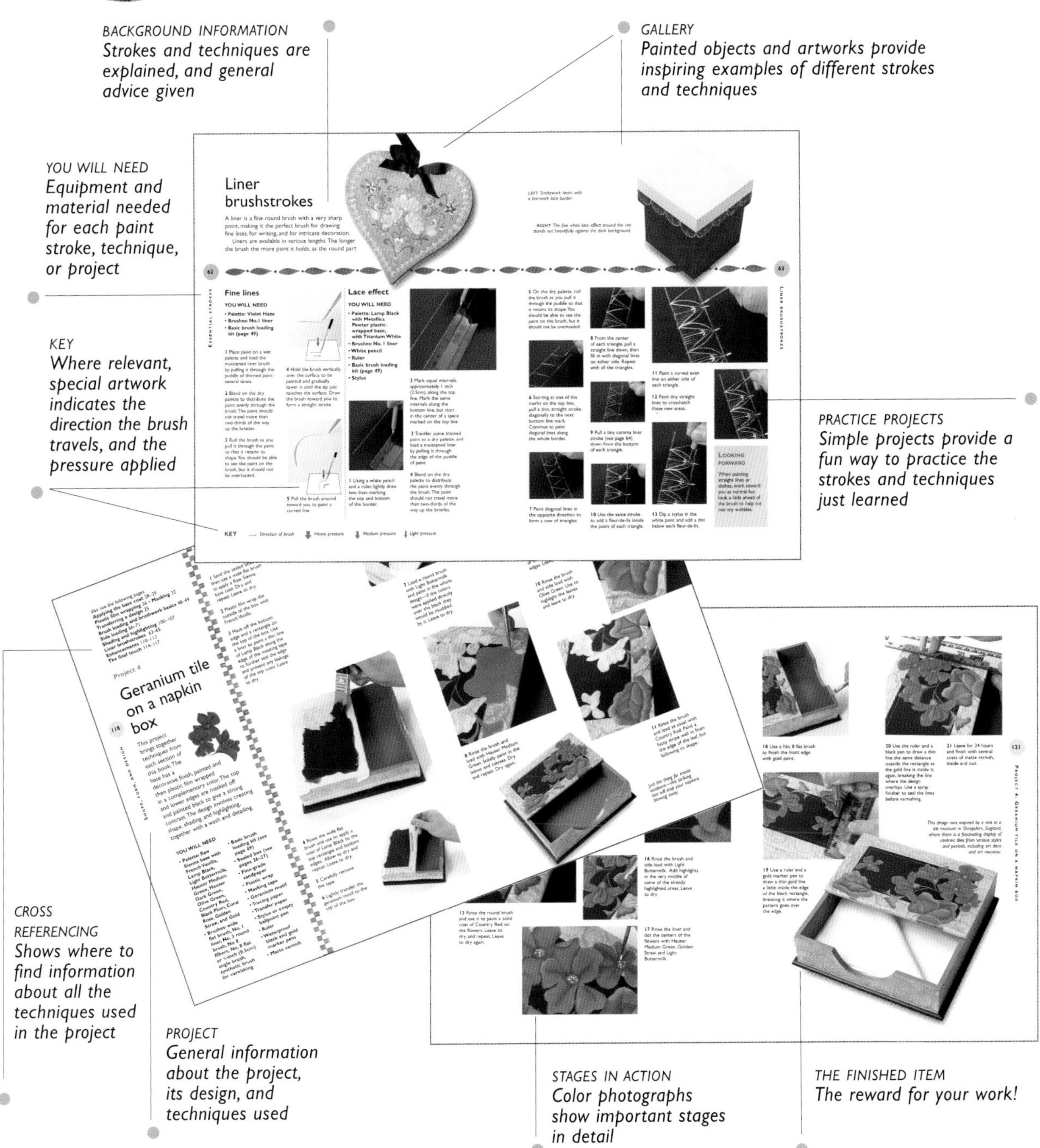

Materials and equipment

There is a vast range of paints and equipment available to decorative painters, though in some parts of the world this may mean using a mail order supplier to get exactly what you want (see Suppliers, page 125). I have listed my preferred paints, mediums, and specialist products. If these are not be available in your area, your local craft store or wood specialist will be able to suggest an alternative.

As you gain experience in painting you will develop your own way of working and build up your own toolbox. Your paint and brushes are your mainstays, so this is not an area in which to economize. When it comes to palettes and other tools, however, there is often an inexpensive alternative, and you can reserve the real thing for your birthday or Christmas list.

Paints and mediums

Acrylic paints are used throughout this book: they are easy to use and equipment used with them can be washed with water. Mediums compatible with acrylic paints have been developed with various properties to make decorative painting easy for everyone.

Acrylic paints

Choose an artist quality acrylic paint, such as DecoArt Americana, or gouache, that is ready-to-use on a moist brush.

A craft paint is another alternative, but you may well have to use several coats to achieve an opaque coverage, whereas an artist quality acrylic paint will cover in a maximum of two.

Retarders

A retarder, such as Easi Float, is mixed with paint or water to give varying drying times, called the "extended open time" because the paint is open for manipulation for an extended period. (Note: some retarders do not mix with water. Be sure to read the manufacturer's instructions.) You can also add a couple of drops of Easi Float to 2 tsp (10ml) of water (your retarder mix) and use this to moisten your brush to aid the flow of paint.

Blending mediums, such as Brush 'n' Blend, are another form of retarder, formulated to work with acrylic paints and used to coat small areas that need to be kept open, or for side loading (see page 66). It has a gel consistency that allows it to stay where you put it without "bleeding." Unlike Easi Float, it is used straight, not in a water mix.

Candle medium

Candle medium can be used straight as a coating on any candle before painting, or added to your chosen color and painted on. The candle should be cleaned first by wiping it with a cloth dampened with surgical spirit (rubbing alcohol), and then allowed to dry.

Fabric medium

Fabric medium can be mixed with acrylic paint to make a durable paint for fabric, but it will not be as hard wearing as fabric paint. Fabric should be washed and dried before being painted. Do not wash with fabric softener, as this stops the paint from sinking into the fabric.

Faux glazing medium

Used to seal the surface after a paint finish or to cover a (dry) design before adding extra detail, this medium ensures that the areas you have already painted are not disturbed by further work.

Paints are available in hundreds of different colors, but you can also mix them to create new ones.

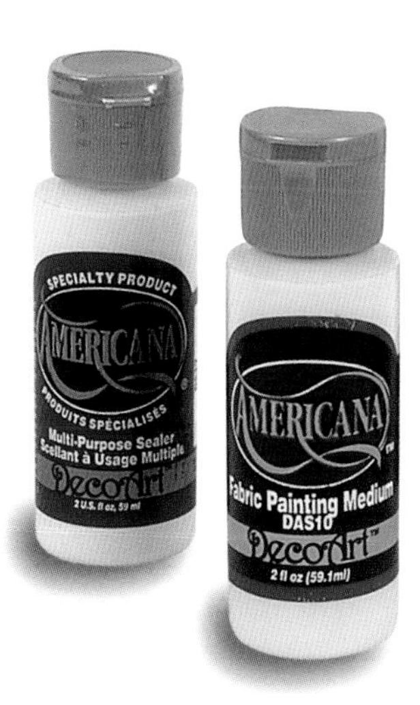

Multipurpose sealer (MPS)

This product is applied directly to a surface to seal it before painting. Multipurpose sealer can also be mixed with equal amounts of base color, allowing you to seal and base coat in one step.

Spray sealer

A spray sealer can be used instead of a brush-on varnish to protect the finish. It is also used to set a paint effect such as a smoked finish (see page 35) and to seal the surface after using a gold marker pen.

Water-based varnishes

Varnishes protect your finished paint effect. A water-based varnish should always be used over acrylic paints to avoid the risk of an adverse reaction. Choose from matte, satin, or gloss finishes, spray- or brush-on. Leave your work for 24 hours before varnishing, and apply several thin coats (see pages 114–115).

There are a variety of mediums for specific purposes.

Crackle medium

Water-based crackle mediums, such as Weathered Wood, are applied between coats of paint to give an almost immediate crackle to the top coat. Top crackle mediums, such as DecoArt's Perfect Crackle, can be painted over the top of your work to give the same effect. A top crackle medium crackles against itself rather than the paint, so the cracks don't become apparant until they are shaded with paint. A dark brown color such as Raw Umber is ideal (see pages 38–39).

Wood filler

Choose a non-shrinking filler for smoothing out dents and holes in your wood before applying the base coat.

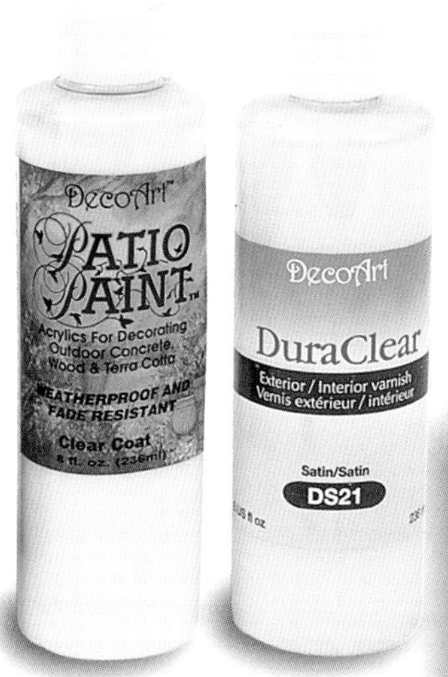

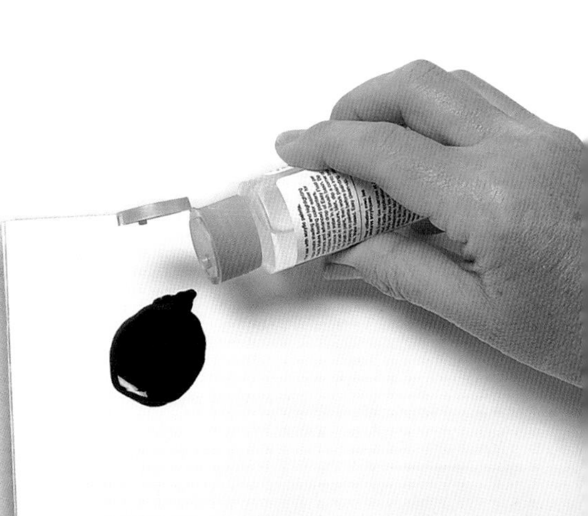

The finishing touches: spray finishes and varnishes.

Brushes

A good starter set should include medium flat, round, and liner brushes. When buying brushes, look for a neat shape. If a brush looks ragged before you paint, it's not going to improve. A good quality synthetic brush will spring back into shape when pressure is released. Buy the best you can afford: you can't produce good strokes with a poor brush.

As you get more adventurous, there is a great variety of special brushes available to add to your brush pot (see pages 86–93), but it is probably better to invest in smaller and larger versions of your basic round and flat brushes before including these.

My choice for a basic set of brushes would be, from the Loew Cornell range, 7000 series Nos 2 and 5, round; 7350 series No. 1, short liner; and 7300 series Nos 6 and 10, shader.

Flat brushes *Liner brushes*

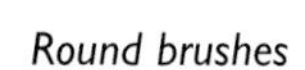
Round brushes

Sponge brushes

A cheap sponge brush with a wooden or plastic handle is ideal for applying base coats and varnish—but don't use the same brush for both!

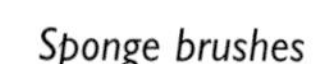
Sponge brushes

Brush maintenance

It is important to clean your brush thoroughly immediately after use. Acrylic paint dries quickly, and dried paint in the bristles will spread them and make it impossible for the brush to return to its original shape. Use a cleaner specially formulated for removing acrylic paint, such as DecoArt DecoMagic.

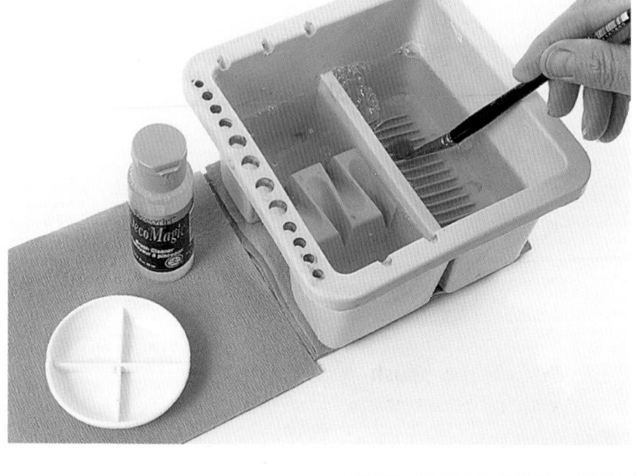

1 Clean your brush in water whenever you put it to one side, even if for a short amount of time. Pull it across the ridged side of a brush basin filled with water, if using one, or a plastic pot scourer in a jar of water (see Brush basin, page 14).

2 Rinse brush in clean water and lay on absorbent paper to drain.

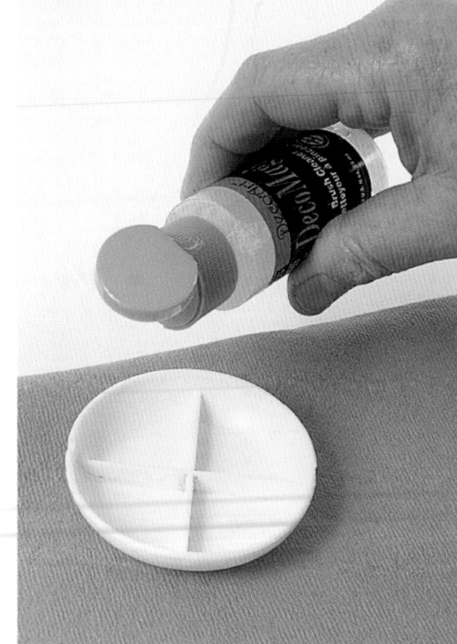

3 When you have finished your painting session, pour a little brush cleaner into a dish.

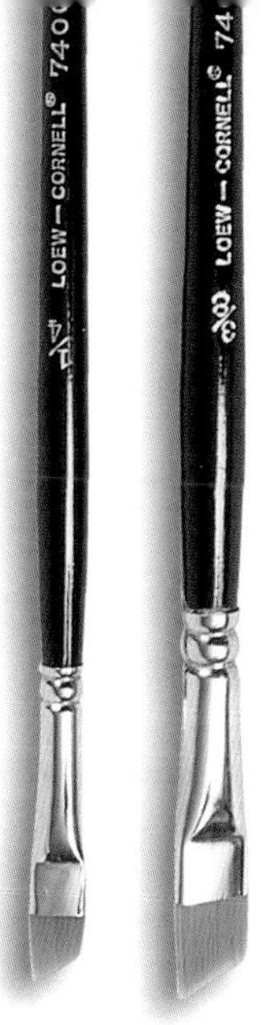

Angle shaders

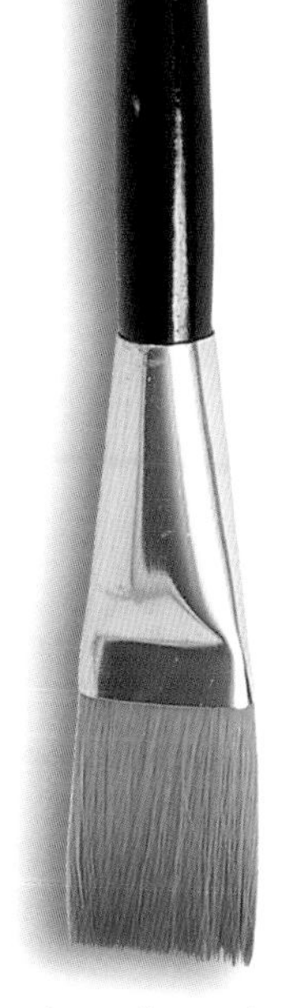

Large flat wash

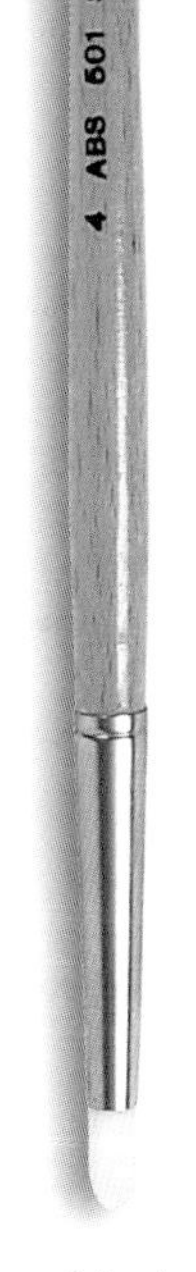

Stippler

Filbert brushes

Comb/rake

Filbert comb/rake

Mops

Cleaning brushes while you work

Add a couple of drops of brush cleaner to the water in your brush basin to help remove paint and keep your brush flexible while you are working. You will still need to clean your brushes properly at the end of the day.

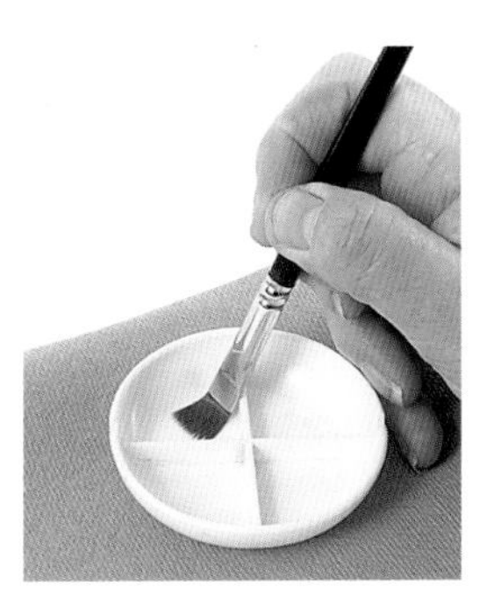

4 Dip your damp brush into the brush cleaner.

5 Holding the end of the bristles in one hand, gently move the brush handle around until the cleaner froths. This clears any paint from under the ferrule.

6 Keep moving the brush as you hold it under cool running water, until all the suds disappear. Dry on a paper towel and reshape with your fingers.

Store brushes with the bristles upright and allow to dry in the open air. Do not put them into an airtight container where they will not dry properly and may go moldy.

Deerfoots

Fan

Stencil brush

Other essentials and economy alternatives

Brush basin

A brush basin is divided into two sections. Brushes are cleaned on the ridged side, and rinsed in fresh water in the other side. Some have added features, such as paint mixing areas. Instead of a commercial brush basin, you could use two jam jars. Put a plastic pot scourer in one to clean the dirty brush and keep the other for rinsing.

Glass or plastic dishes

The base paint—the flat color upon which paint effects and images are applied—and varnish will usually be used in quantities too large for a palette. A household glass or plastic dish is more appropriate. To clean them afterward, follow the steps below.

1 Leave the paint or varnish in the dish to dry out completely.

2 Pour on very hot water and leave for a few seconds.

Brush basin

3 Drain off the hot water, and the remaining paint or varnish will peel off quite easily—the more you have left the easier it is to remove.

Chalk pencil

Gold marker pen

Stylus

Gold marker pen

A gold marker pen, such as a Krylon 18-ct gold marking pen, produces a fast and stylish edge. The fiber tip "holds" your edge, giving a steady line in seconds.

Sandpaper

Small pieces of medium- and fine-grade sandpapers are essential toolbox items. Use the medium grade after sealing and the fine grade for finishing.

Stylus

A stylus is the ideal tool for transferring a design through transfer or tracing paper, and is great for producing dots. However, you could also use an empty ballpoint pen.

Tack cloth

This is a piece of muslin that has been dressed, usually with spirit (alcohol) and linseed oil, and is used to lightly dust the surface after sanding to clear any debris.

Chalk pencil

This is useful for outlining a design directly onto a surface. Also, if you back a traced design with chalk, when you retrace over the design the chalk will transfer onto the surface.

Tracing paper

Tracing paper is used to make a working copy of the design. As it is transparent it is easy to position the design on your surface.

Transfer paper

This is used under a traced pattern to transfer the design to the surface. Various makes and colors are available, but the most useful are white and gray. Transfer paper is fairly expensive to buy but lasts for ages. It only transfers on one side.

Tack cloth

Sandpapers

Tracing paper

Dry palette

Wet palette

Transfer papers

Dry palette

A waxed palette supplies the ideal surface for blending paint. However, you can cover a ceramic tile with plastic wrap and blend on this instead. When it's full, just unwrap the film and throw it away.

Wet palette

Acrylic paints dry out quickly so are best laid out on a damp surface. A good commercial wet palette has an airtight box and special capillary paper that keeps paint workable for weeks. However, a proprietary wet palette is easily imitated with a shallow, airtight plastic box and a piece of damp kitchen sponge cloth.

1 Cut some sponge cloth to the same size as an airtight plastic box lid.

2 Soak the sponge cloth thoroughly in clean water.

3 Squeeze out excess water.

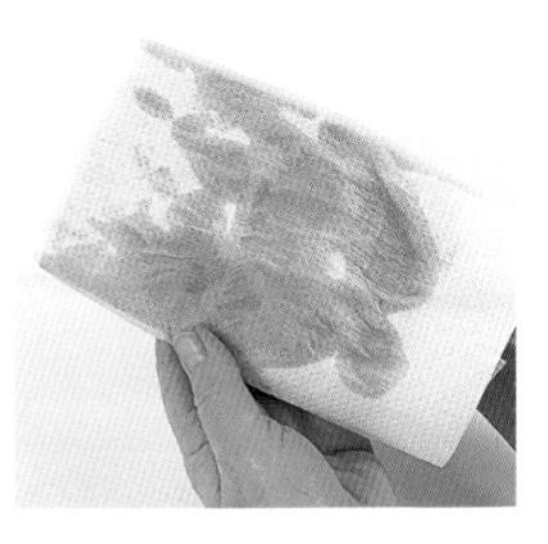

4 Closely wrap a paper towel around the cloth.

5 Place the wrapped cloth on the inside of the box lid and smooth out the paper until no air remains between it and the cloth. Paint can then be placed on the paper.

6 Cover with the bottom of the box when you finish painting and the paint will stay workable for ages.

Useful everyday items

Here are some everyday items that you will find especially useful in your painting kit.

Apron
Cotton swabs
Eraser
Hair dryer
Masking tape
Natural sponge
Old toothbrush
Paper clips
Paper towels
Pencil
Ruler
Scissors
Small palette knife
Small spray bottle—fill with water to mist your palette to prevent it from drying out

Small palette knife

Surfaces and preparation

Painted pieces can be practical and pretty, or purely decorative, and there is an infinite array of surfaces that can be painted—new and old, large and small, from dishes to dustbins, shoeboxes to shed doors. You can paint almost anything! Search a local junk shop, garage sale, or even your own garage or attic and you will find any manner of items that could be the

This decorative ceramic vase is painted with acrylic paints. The background is a plastic film wrap effect (see pages 36–37).

Ceramics and glass

Most ceramics and glass can be painted with conventional acrylic paints over the correct sealer medium, but they will not have the usability of a ceramic item that has been glazed and fired. Therefore, ceramic and glass items painted with acrylics are only useful as decorative objects.

Preglazed ceramics need a special paint, such as DecoArt Ultra Gloss, to adhere to the surface. These pieces do not need sealing but do need to be grease-free before the application of paint. Paint should not be used on surfaces used for food. Keep designs to the edge of plates unless used entirely for decoration. Designs on glasses or mugs should be kept away from the "mouth" area.

Unglazed ceramics or "slipware" are fun to paint on. Clean them with 1:1 vinegar and water before painting. Treat as wood or fiberboard (see page 19), but remember that they cannot be submerged in water, just wiped clean.

Fabric

Cotton and silk are the most usual fabrics to use for painting. Cotton is found in a variety of weights, from fine linen through to heavy calicos and denims. Think about the use of the finished article before choosing your paint. Special fabric paints are available which can be applied straight to the cleaned and dried fabric.

A fabric paint, such as DecoArt So Soft, is ideally suited to soft fabrics and especially clothes: it does not get too stiff. If you are keen to utilize the regular acrylic paints already in your collection, you can use them in conjunction with a textile medium, however the result will be a harder, less flexible finish. This may be appropriate, however, if you are painting a heavy-duty bag or apron.

Wash any fabric items thoroughly before use. Old items need to be clean and free of grease, and new items need to be

A canvas tote bag painted with washable fabric paint.

base for a new work of art. Avoid broken pieces, unless you can repair them yourself or know someone who can do it for you. It takes the gloss off a bargain if you have to spend a fortune getting a piece mended.

Of course, you do need to use the right preparation techniques, sealers, and products for your particular surface, to ensure the best and most longlasting effects. The majority of surfaces you work on will need some preparation. Proper care at this stage will pay dividends later: painting good strokes is much easier on a smooth surface.

washed to remove the dressing (a stiffener used by the fabric manufacturer). Do not use any kind of conditioner, as this coats the fibers and cuts down the absorbency so that the paint tends to sit on top of the fabric rather than soak into it. Make sure the fabric is dry before you begin to paint.

Metal

New tin pieces are often dressed to protect the surface from damage or rusting during transportation and storage. If you have a dishwasher, a full cycle will remove the surface coating. Alternatively, wash the piece carefully with soapy water and dry thoroughly.

Once the piece has dried, it is ready to prime—make sure there is no moisture left in any nooks or crannies. Always use a metal primer (either spray- or brush-on) on metal objects which are to be used outside, and finish with an outdoor varnish. Metal pieces for indoor, dry use can be sealed with a multipurpose sealer. Metal objects can be painted with conventional acrylics if they are sealed beforehand with a multipurpose sealer. Alternatively, you can use a special metal paint.

When using an old metal surface, first remove all traces of rust with a wire brush or wire wool. Treat the metal with a commercial rust inhibitor, following the instructions, before sealing as for new metal.

The base and top of this elegant timepiece are finished in faux marble.

Even an old, or new, oil can may be used as a base for a work of art.

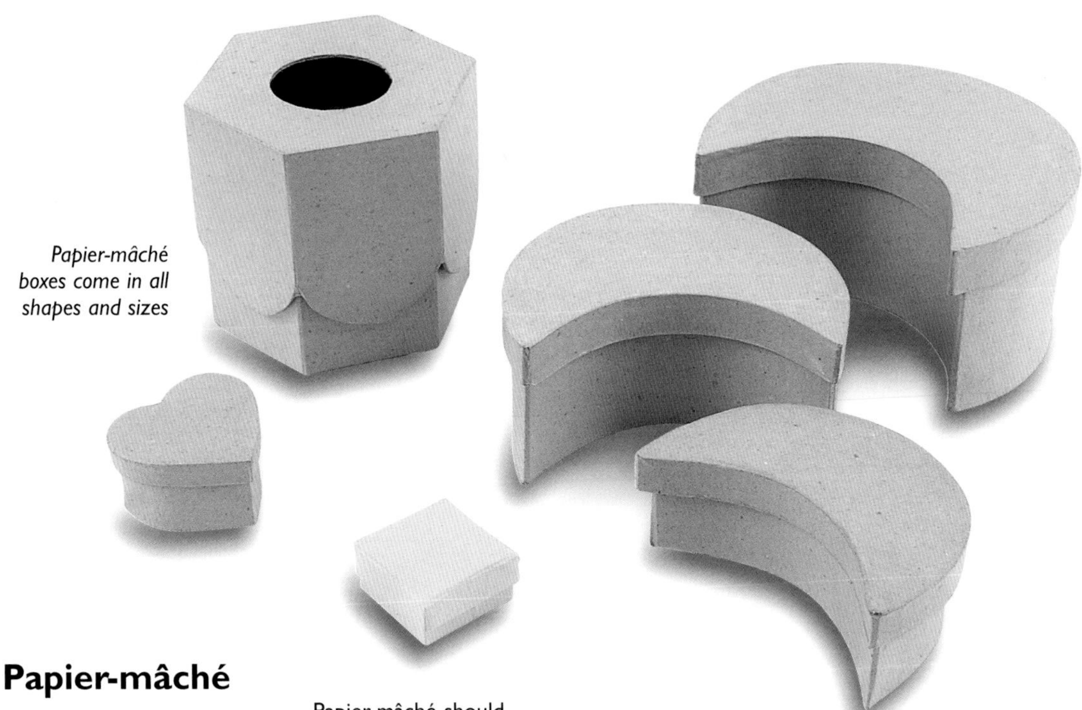

Papier-mâché boxes come in all shapes and sizes

Papier-mâché

This is cheap but can be quite flimsy, and care should be taken when choosing your piece to ensure that it is symmetrical and undamaged. It is not suitable where a robust surface is called for, as it is easily damaged. The uneven surface also makes it unsuitable for stencilling.

Papier-mâché should be treated with a multipurpose sealer before the base coat is applied.

Terra-cotta

Terra-cotta is highly porous, but properly sealed it makes a great, and cheap, surface to paint. Preferably, use only new terra-cotta pots, as the salts in old pots can leech out and affect the adherence of the paint on the surface.

First ensure that pots are clean and dry. Terra-cotta surfaces need to be sealed completely (including the drain hole, if applicable) with a multipurpose sealer. If the slightest amount of moisture penetrates the material, it will lift the paint and destroy all your hard work.

Alternatively, you can use a sealer or a paint specifically designed for porous surfaces, such as DecoArt Patio Paints. These can be painted on directly and give good coverage on the absorbent surface. Properly prepared and varnished pots can be used outside, but it is a good idea to use a liner pot for plants, as scrapes on the inside surface could let moisture in.

Ceramic slipware and terra-cotta pots are very porous, but can easily be painted on once properly sealed.

Wood and medium density fiberboard (MDF)

Various types of wood are easily available, from a light balsa or pine to beech, which is heavier.

If a pine piece has knots showing, a coat of knot sealer, such as Tannin Blocker, will seal the knots and stop any resin leaking out and lifting your painting in the long term. Fill any holes with a non-shrinking wood filler. Sand the surface once it has dried, then apply a multipurpose sealer and sand again with a medium-grade sandpaper. Allow to dry.

Fiberboard is available in a variety of thicknesses and can be easily cut into quite intricate shapes. If cutting fiberboard yourself, always wear a face mask to prevent the inhalation of fine particles.

There is a huge range of medium density fiberboard "blanks" available at most craft stores and through craft magazines and directories. They range from tissue boxes and desks to magazine racks, pedestals and lamp stands.

New wood and fiberboard pieces with a good, smooth surface, will need to be coated with a multipurpose sealer. The sealer raises the grain slightly, so it is best to sand the surface after sealing. Use a medium-grade sandpaper and brush or wipe off any dust before proceeding. Always wear a mask when sanding fiberboard to prevent the fine particles from being inhaled. If the surface is very rough, coat with slightly diluted gesso and dry thoroughly before sanding and sealing.

Old wood pieces can be beautiful but need careful preparation to remove any old polish, varnish, or paint. Use a paint stripper to do this. Follow the manufacturer's instructions, and use in a well-ventilated area, preferably outside. Protect yourself with goggles and rubber gloves since the stripper can burn the skin. For complex shapes, brush the stripper on liberally and wrap the piece in plastic wrap. Leave for 15–30 minutes. The plastic wrap stops the stripper drying out so that it keeps working for longer. Peel off the film and wipe off the loosened paint with newspaper and a wire brush. Repeat if necessary.

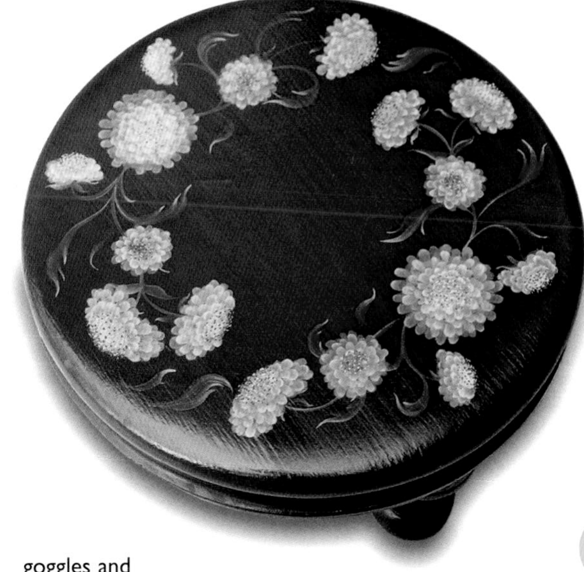

This pretty footstool makes a feature of its wood grain surface.

Flat surfaces can often be cleared of paint by ironing. Heat the iron fully. Place a sheet of good-quality paper, such as a glossy magazine page or discarded letter, on the surface, and hold the iron on it until the paint bubbles. Paint can then be removed with a scraper. Never leave the iron unattended when turned on, but if you do scorch the surface slightly, the marks can be sanded off. Use an old iron, as you probably won't want to iron clothes with it after using it for stripping.

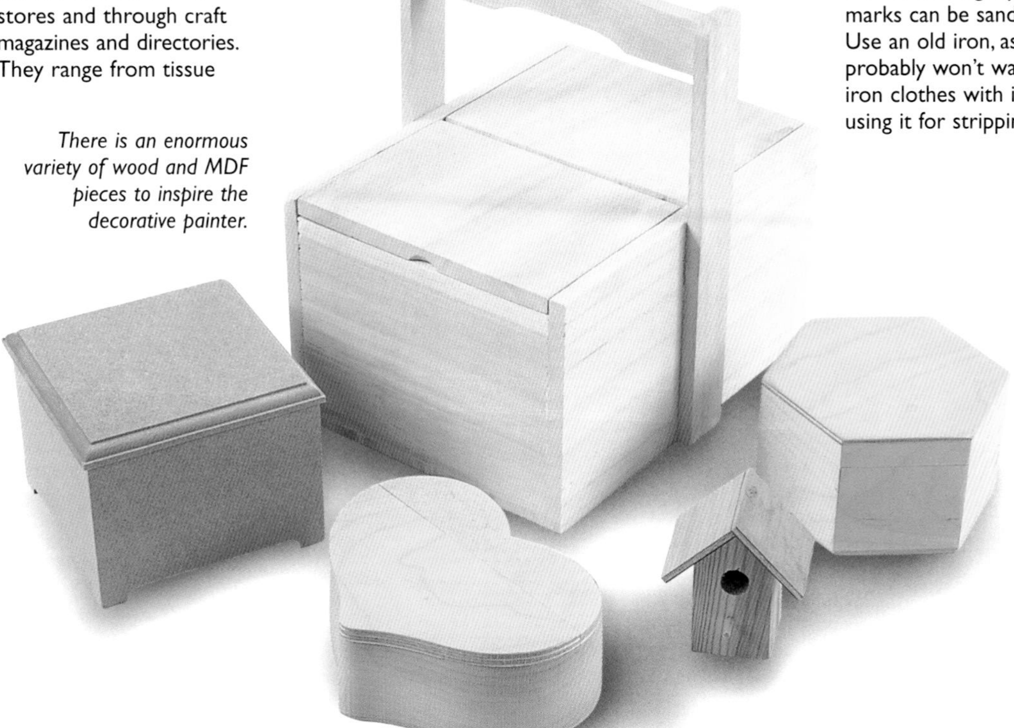

There is an enormous variety of wood and MDF pieces to inspire the decorative painter.

Your workspace

Painting is a pleasure, so don't make it torture by sitting badly and having to constantly stretch for your tools. First choose a place to work in. A table by a window with good daylight is preferable, but strong sunlight can be tiring on the eyes and can "bleach" out colors when you look at them—the paint isn't affected by sunlight, it is just your perception of the colors in very strong light. A north-facing room is ideal for any time of the day, but if you only paint in the afternoon or evening east facing is fine. My studio faces north-west, so I can see the sunlight but it doesn't actually hit the room until late in the day.

If you have to rely on artificial light, make sure it doesn't cast a shadow over your workspace. Portable daylight lamps are available if lighting is a problem. Make sure you have

Layout

Lay your supplies out where you can reach them easily without stretching. The following suggestions are for a right-handed painter. Reverse everything if you are left-handed.

This is how I work, but I have laid it out purely as a guide: try it and adapt the layout to work for you. If you are painting a deep object, such as a large box, it may be easier to work on your lap, but you will still find this layout useful.

Place your brush holder to the left. This holder is a piece of wood drilled with holes in various sizes and depths. You can buy holders of various shapes and sizes, and these are very useful if you travel to classes, but I find I can see my brushes easily in this.

Keep a hair dryer on the far left, ready to dry work as you go. Sometimes, I move it away from my work area deliberately, so that I have to stand up. Sometimes I get so involved in painting I don't move for hours, which is not good for the circulation.

Keep transfer paper, tracing paper, patterns, and masking tape on the left, to have them handy when you need them.

Position a piece of blue paper towel in front of you to place the surface being painted on. The color allows you to try out light floats and stipples and see how much paint is on the brush, impossible on a white tile or palette.

your eyes tested regularly—you won't be able to do fine lining work if you can't see the end of your brush.

A rigid table with plenty of space for your supplies is essential. A wobbly table will get extremely irritating, especially if you start to erase something vigorously and spill water over your work.

Next, choose your chair. It should be low enough for you to rest your forearms on the table without lifting your shoulders, but not so low that you have to lean forward. Do not cross your legs, as this immediately raises one shoulder and puts strain on your back. Place your feet flat on the floor or cross your ankles.

It is a good idea to cover your work area (and beyond) with a protective covering. Look in the local garden center for thick waterproof plastic—it's very cheap and makes an ideal cover.

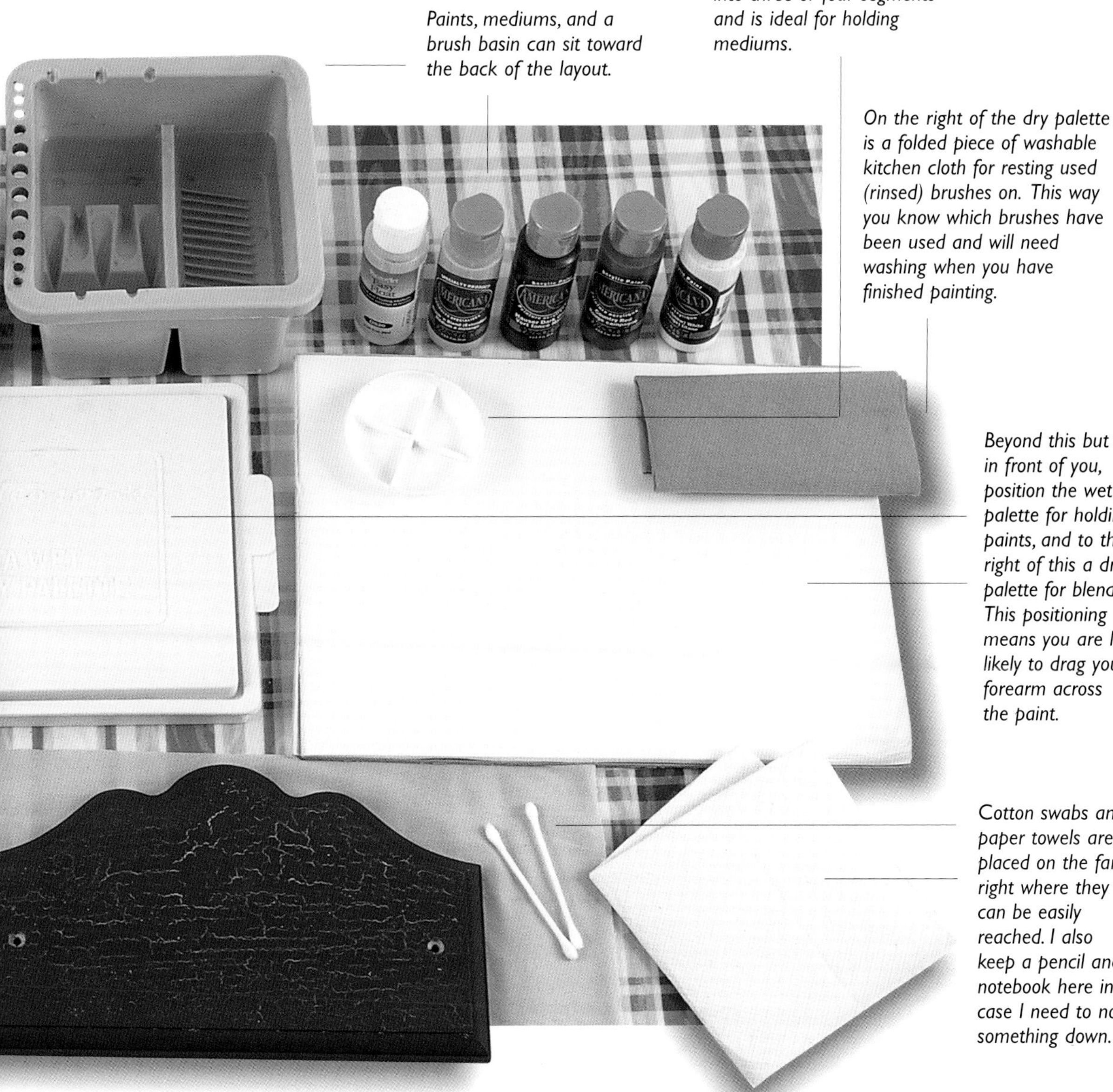

Paints, mediums, and a brush basin can sit toward the back of the layout.

A tinting dish rests on the dry palette. This is divided into three or four segments and is ideal for holding mediums.

On the right of the dry palette is a folded piece of washable kitchen cloth for resting used (rinsed) brushes on. This way you know which brushes have been used and will need washing when you have finished painting.

Beyond this but still in front of you, position the wet palette for holding paints, and to the right of this a dry palette for blending. This positioning means you are less likely to drag your forearm across the paint.

Cotton swabs and paper towels are placed on the far right where they can be easily reached. I also keep a pencil and notebook here in case I need to note something down.

GETTING STARTED

GETTING STARTED

Once you have set up a comfortable workspace and prepared your surface, it is time to start thinking about your design and the background on which you want it set. First a base coat should be applied, and then there are any number of decorative paint effects to choose from.

Patterns and designs

There are hundreds of books and magazines featuring a wide range of decorative patterns, available in craft stores, studios, and by mail order. You will soon home in on an artist whose style and technique suits you and provides you with an endless source of inspiration. The success of your finished piece depends, in part, on your choice of design and how it is positioned and proportioned on the surface. It is also a good idea to take some time deciding the size, background, and colors you are going to use. The colors may be determined by the

Choosing a pattern

Here is a checklist of things to bear in mind when choosing your design:

- **The size and shape of the design compared with the surface.**
- **The use of the piece.**
- **The look you want to achieve. For example, is it to be an all-over pattern or confined to a small part of the surface? Will the design be repeated, totally or in part, on another face of the piece?**
- **The balance between a previous painted finish and the design. For example, a complicated all-over pattern could get lost on a strongly contrasted paint effect background.**

Adjusting the size

When you have decided on the size of design you need, you will probably want to enlarge or reduce the original. If you have access to a photocopier it is easy to copy the design in several sizes to decide which you prefer. Alternatively, a child's pantograph gives an accurate copy of your design and you can adjust the size by dividing or multiplying the size of the pattern to fit the surface. If neither of these are available, simply use a grid pattern to adjust the size.

1 Draw up a regimented grid of squares over the motif you want to increase or decrease in size.

2 Draw a second regimented grid onto a clean sheet of paper, making the squares bigger or smaller to correspond with the final size you want to achieve. Copy the design, square by square, onto the second grid.

Borders

Think about adding a border—this can look especially striking on a large piece. For example, you could either mask off an evenly proportioned edge all around and add a toning paint effect, or add a simple border of plain comma strokes.

Here the border is provided by the edge of the tray itself, painted gold and emphasized by the lacework cornices.

Adapting a design

Of course, you don't have to use the whole design.

1 Trace the design, or enlarge or reduce it, and cut out its main components.

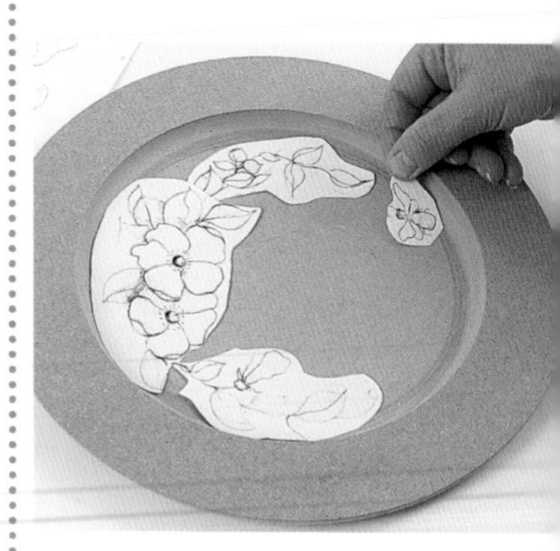

2 Arrange the pieces on the surface to be painted to form a pleasing design. Remember, your eye is the best guide to what looks right and what looks wrong.

pattern you have chosen. If, for example, it is a prepresented design from a book or magazine, you may only need to make slight alterations to change the tone and make it more fitting to the situation of the finished piece.

LEFT This wall-mounted candle holder is decorated with a generous bow and double-loaded rosebuds.

RIGHT The linerwork lace and faux ribbon make a beautiful edge for this fan-shaped box.

Transferring a design

Tracing a design onto translucent paper saves wear and tear on the original, and also makes it easier to position the pattern on your surface. Only trace the main pattern lines. Any intricate work is best done freehand so that it does not look too stiff or regimented.

Using transfer paper

1 Place a traced motif onto the surface and anchor with a couple of small pieces of masking tape.

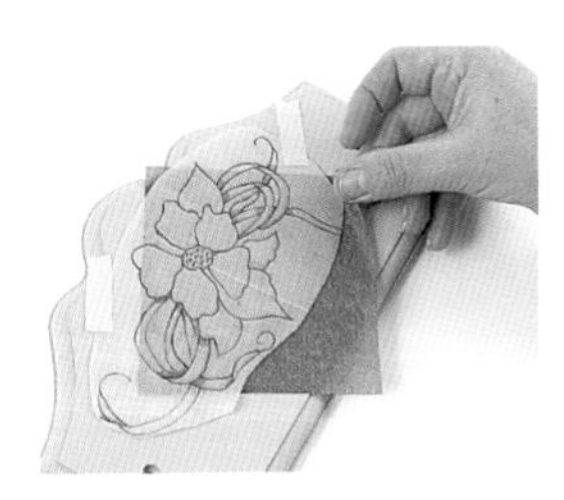

2 Choose a piece of transfer paper in a contrasting color to the base and slip it under the tracing.

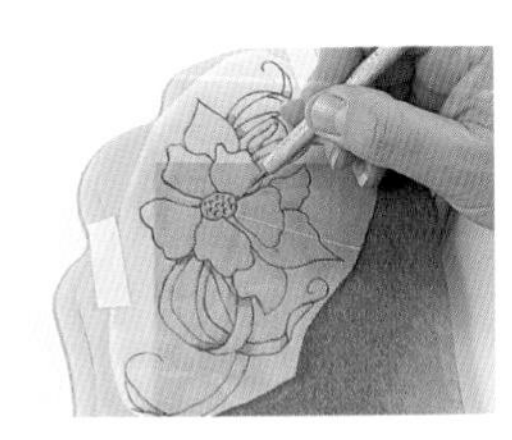

3 Trace over the design using a stylus or empty ballpoint pen, moving the transfer paper as required.

4 When the papers are removed, the design is clearly visible on the base.

Using tracing paper

1 If you do not have transfer paper at hand, you can rub chalk into the back of your tracing, using a color that contrasts with the base.

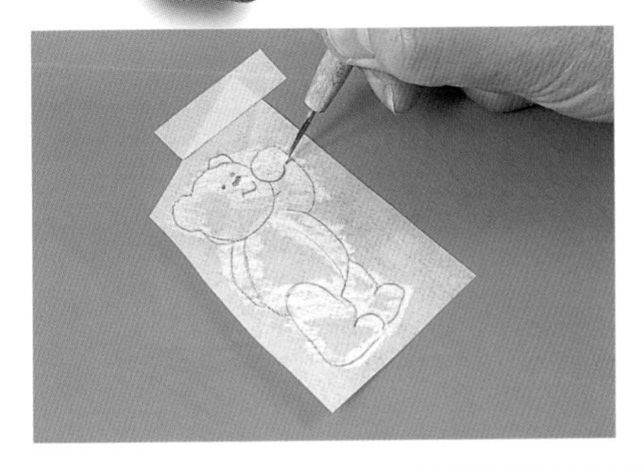

2 Fix the tracing to the base with masking tape, chalk side down. Trace over the motif again with a stylus or empty ballpoint pen.

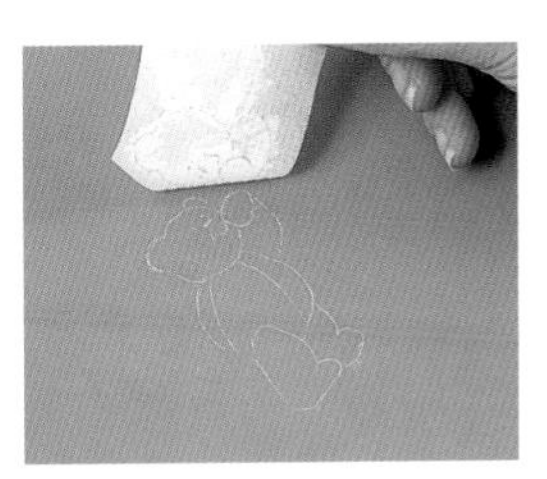

3 When you remove the tracing the motif can be clearly seen on the base. The disadvantage of this transferring method is that the chalk rubs away when you touch it and can leave a grainy residue. For light colored surfaces, pencil is an alternative, but this can also smudge.

Which way up

Transfer paper can only be used one way up. Put a tiny dab of paint on the top side of the paper and you will always instantly know which way to use it.

Avoiding smudges

When using a new piece of dark transfer paper, rub the colored side with a paper towel to remove excess carbon and prevent smudging.

Making your own designs

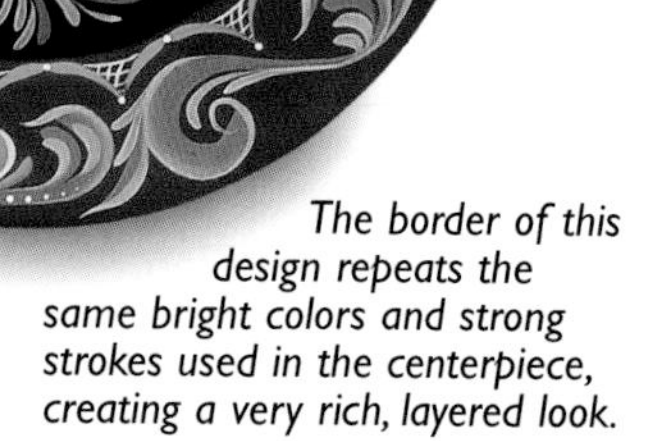

Once you have practised the basics of decorative painting, using patterns from books and magazines, you will probably want to start designing for yourself.

Look for inspiration all around you, bearing in mind that anything you see or collect can be adapted into your own,

The border of this design repeats the same bright colors and strong strokes used in the centerpiece, creating a very rich, layered look.

Drawing up your design

Having chosen a subject and a base surface, you will need to decide on a shape for the design that will fit the space available on the base.

A corner design

1 Add some specific elements to your basic motif so that it looks comfortable in a corner position. First draw the motif, such as this simple flower.

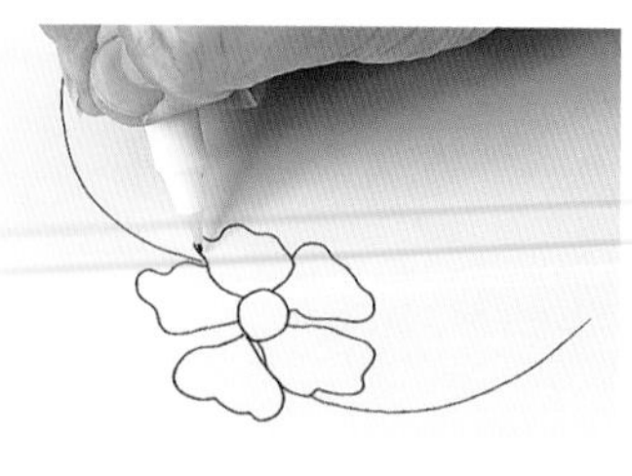

2 Pull a curve out from each side, roughly at right angles.

3 Add leaves and buds to the curves to give a balanced design.

4 The basic original motif now specifically fits its corner placement. Here it has been painted on a book cover that was first treated with a coat of multipurpose sealer.

A circular design

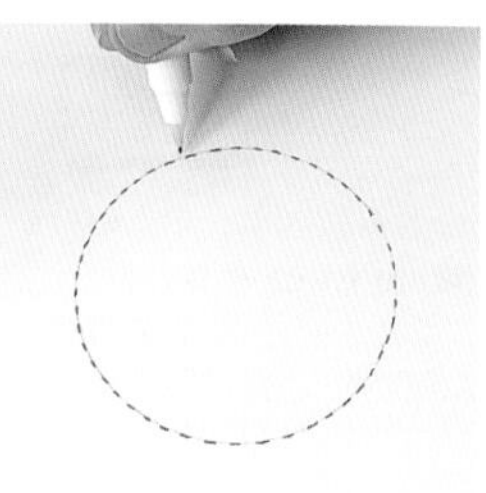

1 Draw a circle that corresponds to the size you want the design to be on the finished piece.

2 Draw three simple motifs, such as flowers, at equal distances around the circle.

A variation of the main design on the lid of the box is repeated in panels on the front and side.

individual design. Look out for images or photographs in books or magazines that attract you. You may also find inspiration in greetings cards and wrapping paper, or even your own photographs. Pick out elements or colors you can use, and adapt them to your own specifications.

3 Add leaves and buds between the flowers to give a balanced design. You can add more and more detail to develop the design, simply working around the initial ring.

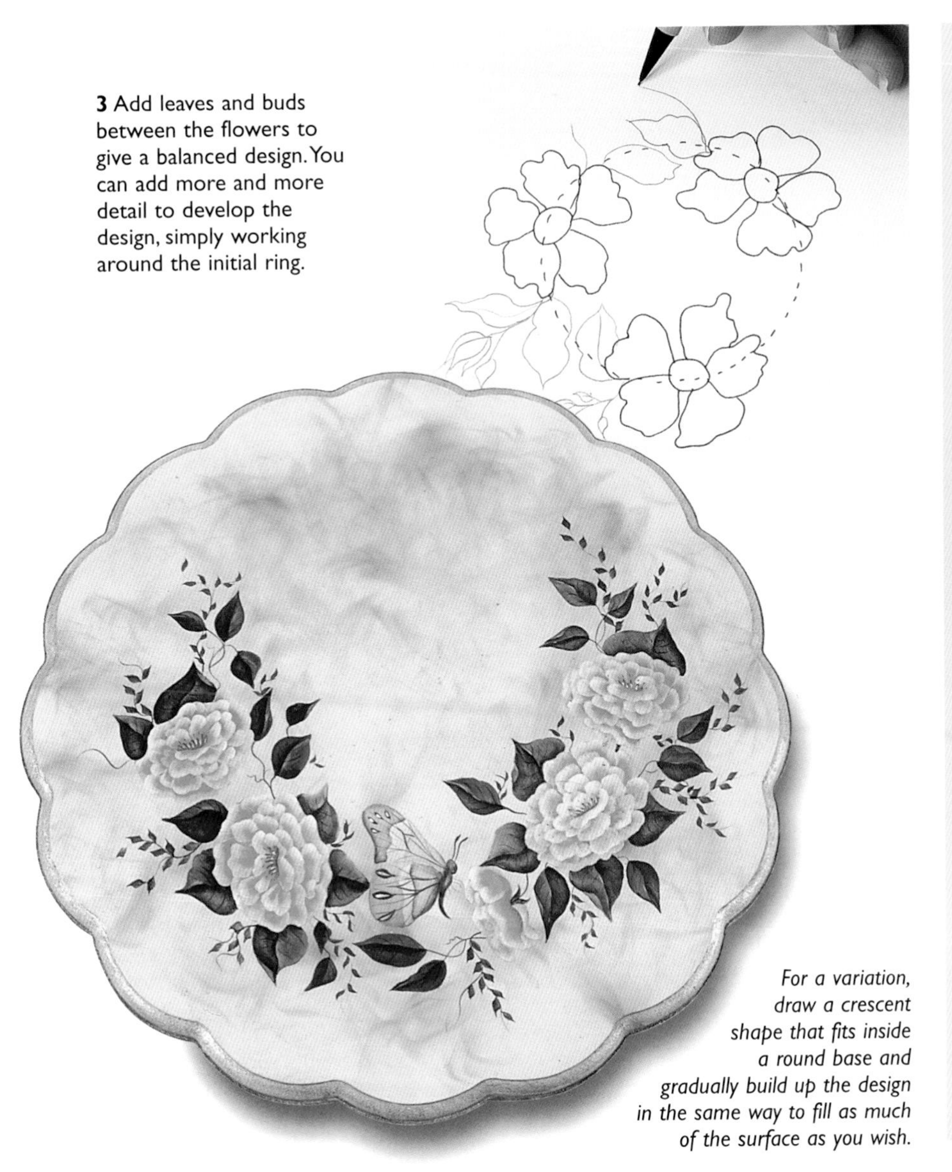

For a variation, draw a crescent shape that fits inside a round base and gradually build up the design in the same way to fill as much of the surface as you wish.

Color

As you practise and experiment you will soon find combinations of colors that you specifically prefer. Here are a few tips to boost your confidence in using color, to help you get started.

- **For floral designs, when the main design colors are yellow, orange, or scarlet, choose greens with a yellow tint.**
- **Choose greens with a blue tint when working with blues, purples, or burgundy reds.**
- **Use a thin wash of a flower color to tint a leaf to give a design cohesion.**
- **If you look closely at animal fur, you will see a myriad of colors in what may have looked like simple gray. Thin washes of these other colors make the results more realistic.**

The base coat

The base coat is the starting point for most decorative painting images. "Basing," also known as "color blocking," provides the flat color that covers your surface before specific paint finishes or motifs are applied. Normal acrylic colors are suitable for the base coat, which is applied simply with a fully loaded brush, coat upon coat. Aerosol spray paints are also an option, but care is required to minimize

A child's pull-along toy carriage. The clouds are painted using a side-load technique.

Applying the base coat

Most surfaces will be coated with a sealer before the base coat is applied. One exception is wood stains. They are designed to absorb into the wood, and can be applied straight onto a bare wood surface.

1 Make sure the piece is clean and grease-free before applying an even coat of multipurpose sealer with a paintbrush. Allow to dry.

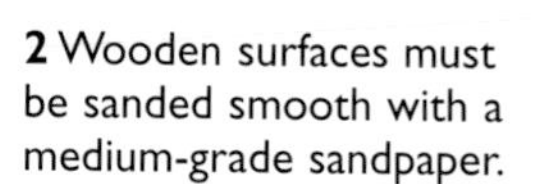

2 Wooden surfaces must be sanded smooth with a medium-grade sandpaper.

USING A HAIR DRYER TO SPEED THE DRYING PROCESS

Keep the hair dryer at least 12 inches (30cm) away from the surface and remove as soon as the surface is dry. Too much heat can make the paint bubble up. Make sure the surface has cooled completely before applying the next coat as any residual heat will dry the paint you apply too quickly, causing uneven strokes.

This base coat on this waste paper bin forms a part of the overall picture.

"overspray" onto neighboring areas, and they should only be used in well-ventilated areas. All aerosols are best used outside on a still day.

Most paints will require two or three coats, but if you are basing a dark surface with a light pigment, you may need more. Don't be afraid to mix colors to get exactly the shade you want, but bear in mind while mixing that the paint will dry darker.

FLUFF FREE

Never wear a fluffy jumper when you are painting or varnishing. The tiny fibers waft around in the air and invariably some will land on your wet surface. If the worst happens, wait until the surface is dry but not "set," and gently scratch the fiber free with a fingernail. Retarders in particular seem to attract fluff.

3 Wipe off any residue with a tack cloth.

4 Use a wide, flat paintbrush or a foam brush to apply your base paint. Brush on evenly and smooth out any streaks. Remember that two thin coats are much better than one thick one. Check round all the corners to make sure there are no drips. Leave to dry completely. Sand lightly with fine sandpaper and remove dust before applying another coat: some colors may need coating for a third time.

The design on this recipe holder and tea towel rack is painted onto a dark base coat, creating a gingham effect where masking with white has been applied *(see page 32–33).*

Paint effects

Before transferring a design, consider the background. Do you want a plain, solid color, or would a more decorative finish show off your piece to greater advantage?

A paint effect, from subtle washes to sponging and crackling, gives interest to a background. Some of the finishes can be effective on their own. For example,

This graded wash background sees the blue sky fading into the green ground.

Single color wash

A washed finish should be very soft, with color and shade changing gradually. The key word here is "subtle." The effect is achieved by applying slightly diluted paint over an already damp surface.

YOU WILL NEED

- **Palette: Antique White base with Uniform Blue wash**
- **Brushes: 2 wide brushes**
- **Prepared base (see pages 28–29)**
- **Tinting dish**
- **Easi Float retarder**
- **Wet palette**
- **Dry palette**

1 In a tinting dish, dilute eight drops of retarder in 1 tbsp (15ml) of water.

2 Dip a wide brush into the retarder mix and brush it across the surface to be washed. Repeat several times, as the surface will absorb some of the liquid. The surface should glisten, but not be running with water. This process can be done one side at a time on a large object, but check carefully for drips on the surfaces that have already been worked on.

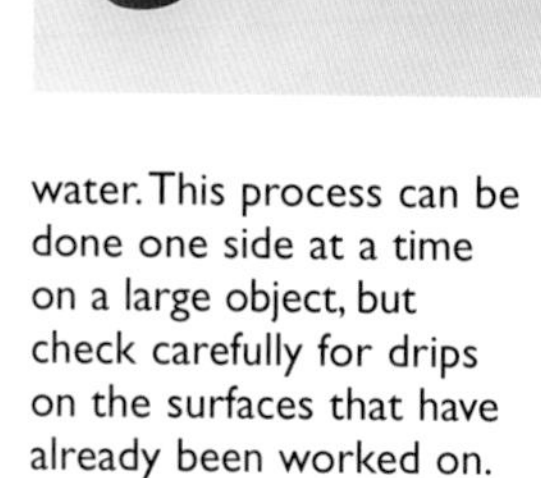

3 Transfer some acrylic paint to a wet palette. Pick up a tiny amount of paint on a clean brush and mix it into a small puddle of water on a dry palette.

4 Apply the slightly diluted paint to the damp surface in long, even strokes. Leave to dry thoroughly before repeating, if required, or painting a design.

Blended multicolor wash

This more complex technique is still based on the wash—applying lightly diluted paint to a damp surface—and produces a very subtly tinted finish.

YOU WILL NEED

- **Palette: Antique White base with Admiral Blue, Country Blue and Avocado tints**
- **Brushes: wide brush, round brush, fan brush**
- **Prepared base (see pages 28–29)**
- **Easi Float retarder**
- **Tinting dish**
- **Wet palette**
- **Dry palette**
- **Damp cloth**

1 Mix equal amounts of retarder and water in a tinting dish and use a wide brush to coat the

to complement the design on a lid, the base of a box could simply be plastic wrapped in two colors from the design. Other, more subtle, finishes, such as a sponged effect, look better when "dressed" with a design.

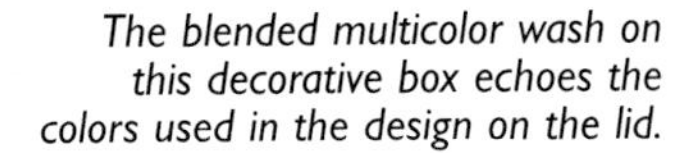

The blended multicolor wash on this decorative box echoes the colors used in the design on the lid.

surface with the mixture. Apply a few coats, as the surface will absorb some of the liquid. The surface should glisten but not be running with water. On large objects, check carefully for drips on the surfaces that have already been worked on.

2 Transfer some acrylic paint to a wet palette. Pick up a little of the first color on a round brush and blend it on a dry palette with a little water or retarder mix.

3 Smudge the diluted color gently onto the damp surface in random areas.

4 Clean the brush and repeat step 3 with the remaining colors, taking care not to overpaint two colors.

5 Use a fan brush to gently blend each color into the background and into each other.

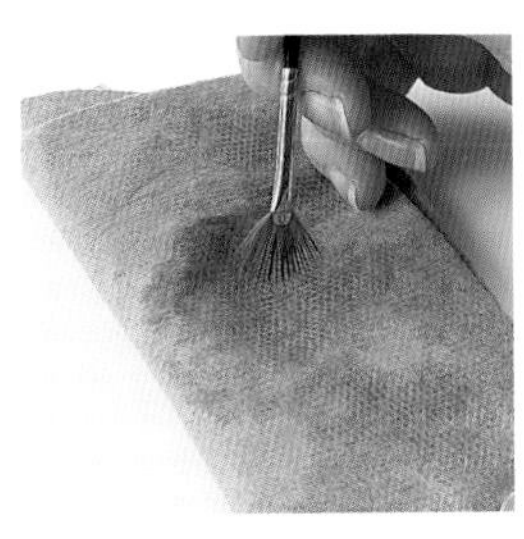

6 Wipe the brush frequently on a damp cloth to avoid muddying the colors.

7 Continue blending with the fan brush until the colors merge seamlessly into each other. Leave the background to dry thoroughly before proceeding with your design: this may take as much as 24 hours unless you use a hair dryer.

An infinite number of effects can be obtained by using different colors with any of the finishes discussed. Make up some color boards using different combinations, light over dark, dark over light, add two or more colors, try adding a final touch with gold—the possibilities are endless. Look at the main colors of your chosen design and pick out two or three, then try using them in different sequences. Each sequence will give an

Sponging

One of the simplest paint finishes is sponging. In its basic form, sponging uses a sponge to apply a single color to a prepainted background. Of course, more interest can be added by using two or more colors that complement each other. Different effects can also be obtained depending on the type of sponge you use, natural or synthetic, close-textured or open. Experiment and choose the result that best suits your design.

YOU WILL NEED

- **Palette: Lilac base with Royal Blue and Titanium White**
- **Brushes: liner (optional)**
- **Prepared base (see pages 28–29)**
- **Masking tape (optional)**
- **Scissors (optional)**
- **Wet palette**
- **Natural sponge**
- **Dry palette**
- **Paper towel**

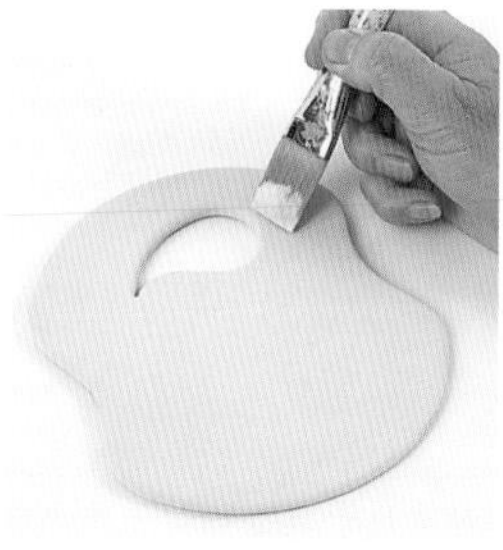

1 Transfer some acrylic paint to a wet palette. With a damp sponge, pick up a little of the first color. Work the paint further into the sponge on a dry palette.

2 Dab off excess paint on a paper towel.

3 Press the sponge evenly over the surface. Reload with paint as necessary and change the sponge when it becomes saturated with paint. Leave to dry.

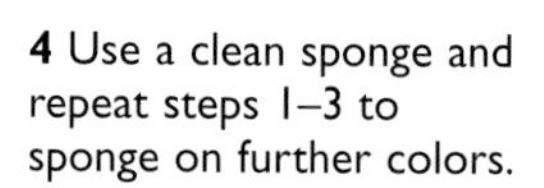

4 Use a clean sponge and repeat steps 1–3 to sponge on further colors.

5 Finally, pick up a little of the base color on a clean sponge and apply lightly over the surface. The addition of the base color will soften the overall look.

6 Allow to dry completely before carefully removing the masking tape and adding your design.

REVERSE COLORS

Try using the colors in this palette in the reverse order, so that two shades of blue are sponged over a buttermilk base, for a totally different look.

Masking

Sections of a surface can be divided off with tape that masks that area from paint. Masking tape, available in varying widths, can be applied to a surface in any number of shapes, and the unmasked areas either painted flat or given a paint effect.

YOU WILL NEED

- **Palette: White base with Hauser Dark Green**
- **Brushes: liner (optional), wide brush**
- **Prepared base (see pages 28–29)**
- **Masking tape**
- **Natural sponge**
- **Scissors**
- **Wet palette**

***RIGHT** Masked vertical stripes work well on the round form of this hat box to create a fun candy-stripe effect.*

***LEFT** Dark brown sponging has been used on this box to create a convincing wood effect.*

1 Cut masking tape strips to size and press onto the prepared surface.

2 Run your thumbnail along the edge of the tape to ensure the paint does not seep under the tape.

3 You could paint a thin line of the base color along the edge of the masking tape to seal the edge and prevent any leakage of the top color.

4 Transfer some paint to the wet palette. With a damp sponge, pick up a little of the first color. Work the paint into the sponge on a dry palette.

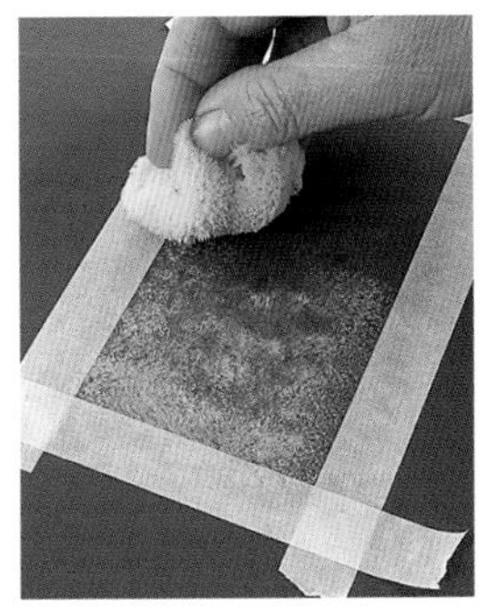

5 Now, simply paint or sponge in the unmasked area. Any paint that is brushed onto the tape will be removed when the tape is lifted to reveal the perfect painted shape. You can also use any of the finishes described in this section to fill in the unmasked area.

6 Leave the paint to completely dry before carefully removing the tape and continuing with your design.

Stripes

Following on from masking, interesting backgrounds can be produced using masking tape to form regular shapes on your surface.

YOU WILL NEED

- **Palette: Light French Blue base**
- **Brushes: liner (optional), wide brush**
- **Prepared base (see pages 28–29)**
- **Masking tape**
- **Scissors**
- **Wet palette**

1 To make a simple stripe, lay strips of masking tape next to each other across your surface.

MAKING STANDARD MASKING TAPE "LOW-TACK"

When using a standard masking tape, as opposed to a low-tack variety, press the tacky side of the tape on your apron before positioning it. This process will take some of the "tack" or stickiness off the tape so that it is less likely to pull paint up when it is removed.

2 Peel off alternate pieces of tape to reveal the unmasked stripes.

3 Follow steps 5–6 of Masking.

RIGHT *Stippling has been used here to create a background foliage effect.*

BELOW *A stippler brush has been used to paint the purple flower in the top corner, giving it a "wispy" look. See page 86 for this technique.*

Stippling

This effect is similar to sponging (see pages 32–33) but gives a more regular finish. Stippling is only really suitable for small areas, since it is quite hard work. The stippling brush has a domed head, which is dabbed lightly, or "pounced," on the surface to create heavy dots.

YOU WILL NEED

- **Palette: Celery Green base with Moon Yellow**
- **Brushes: liner (optional), stippling brush or small stencil brush**
- **Prepared base (see pages 28–29)**
- **Masking tape (optional)**
- **Scissors (optional)**
- **Wet palette**
- **Dry palette**
- **Paper towel**

1 Prepare to work this effect on a small area, or mask off a shape to be stippled on a larger prepared surface.

2 Transfer some acrylic paint to a wet palette. Pick up some paint on a stippling brush and work the paint into the brush on a dry palette.

3 Dab the brush on a paper towel until most of the paint is removed.

4 Hold the brush vertically and dab the bristles evenly all over the surface.

5 Leave the paint to dry completely before carefully removing the tape and continuing with your design.

individual look. As you gain more experience, you can also try combining paint finishes.

If you are covering the entire piece with a pattern, a paint effect may be much too busy, but if your design only covers a small proportion of the surface area, a special finish in toning colors could enhance it.

You may find that you are so pleased with your paint finish you don't want to paint over it and have to rethink the positioning and size of your design.

The pale gray background with a smoked finish tones well with the mauves of the design on this dainty box.

Smoked finish

The smoked effect is the only background texture that is not finished with paint. Instead, it relies on natural smoke to pattern the base. This effect could also be used over another paint finish that uses subtle colors. The process of holding the base and a knife over a candle flame can be a bit like rubbing your tummy while patting you head, but you'll soon get the hang of it. Practice on a piece of card first.

YOU WILL NEED

- **Palette: Dove Grey base**
- **Brushes: wide brush**
- **Sealed base (see page 28)**
- **Candle and matches**
- **Metal knife, used solely for paint techniques**

1 Apply a base coat to the surface and allow to dry. Smoking should be done as soon as the base painting is dry so that the smoke can sink into the paint.

2 Light a candle and hold a metal knife in the flame at a 45° angle, adjusting the height of the knife until smoke rises. Keep your hand well away from the flame.

3 With the knife still over the flame, hold the base in your other hand and turn it so that the area to be smoked is directly over the smoke, but well away from the flame. Move the base around so that the smoke touches the whole area.

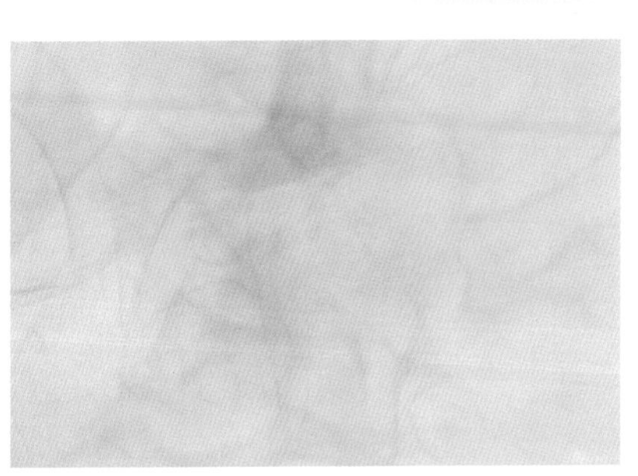

4 Leave to dry overnight before adding your design.

Glass coasters with plastic wrap background design. The shades of blue have been reversed to add variety within the set.

Toweling off

The technique of toweling off gives a very textured finish. The example given uses paper towel, but other materials can be used to create different effects. You can also use the "towel" to apply the paint rather than take it off. Spreading a piece of cheesecloth across the paint, pressing down and then peeling it carefully off will give a clear impression of the texture of the cloth. Using it scrunched up will give a very soft finish.

YOU WILL NEED

- **Palette: Buttermilk base with Hauser Dark Green**
- **Brushes: wide brush**
- **Prepared base (see pages 28–29)**
- **Tinting dish**
- **Easi Float retarder**
- **Paper towel**

1 In a tinting dish, mix two to three drops of retarder in 2 tsp (10ml) of acrylic paint.

2 Load a wide brush with treated acrylic paint and coat the prepared base thoroughly.

3 Scrunch up a piece of paper towel and dab it evenly all over the still-wet paint, picking off the top color in places. Work from one side of the surface to the other, trying not to make the pattern too regimented.

4 Rescrunch or change the towel when its surface becomes covered in paint, revealing a clean face to towel off with.

5 Leave the background to thoroughly dry before proceeding with your design.

Plastic film wrapping

Plastic film wrapping can be completed in two or more colors. The use of a retarder in the paint gives the artist time to make adjustments before it dries. However, you then have to wait a long time for it to dry so that you can paint over it.

YOU WILL NEED

- **Palette: Buttermilk base with Hauser Dark Green**
- **Brushes: wide brush**
- **Prepared base (see pages 28–29)**
- **Tinting dish**
- **Easi Float retarder**
- **Plastic wrap**

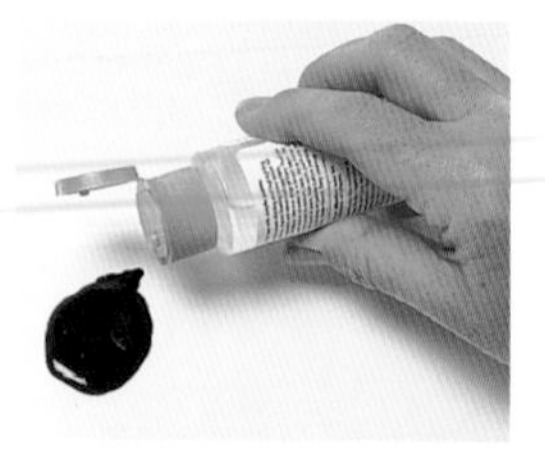

1 In a tinting dish, mix four to six drops of retarder in 2 tsp (10ml) of Hauser Dark Green.

For those special words—this notecard has a sponge crackled background in black and gold, with round-brush daises as the main design.

2 Load a wide brush with the treated paint and coat the base thoroughly.

3 Scrunch up a generous piece of plastic wrap, straighten it out slightly, then press it down on the surface of the still-wet paint.

4 Gently move around the resulting pleats and folds in the wrap with your fingers to give an even coverage.

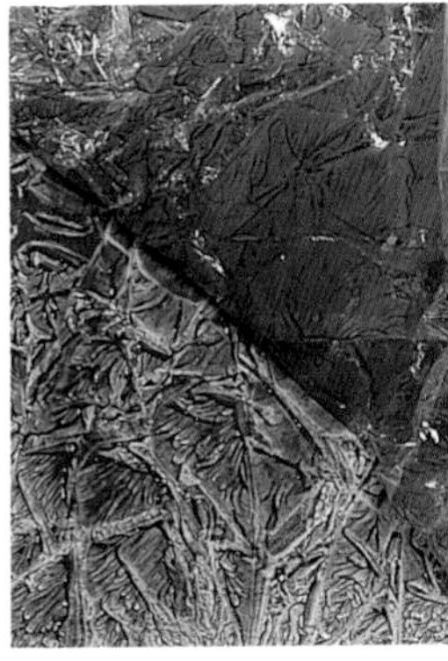

5 Hold the base still and carefully peel back the plastic film, working toward you from one corner. Repeat all over the wet paint, slightly overlapping the plastic film over previous wrapped areas to avoid creating join lines. Replace the plastic film as it becomes saturated with paint.

6 Leave the paint to completely dry before continuing with your design.

Sponge crackle

One way to achieve an "aged" look is to apply a crackle medium to the paintwork.

YOU WILL NEED

- **Palette: Admiral Blue base with Dove Grey**
- **Brushes: wide brush**
- **Prepared base (see pages 28–29)**
- **Crackle medium**
- **Tinting dish**
- **Dry palette**
- **Natural sponge**

1 Pour a little crackle medium into a tinting dish. Load a wide brush with crackle medium and brush it evenly over the prepared surface. The thicker the application, the larger the cracks will be. Allow to dry.

2 Transfer some acrylic paint to a palette and load a natural sponge generously with paint. Working on one surface area at a time, sponge the top color over the dry crackle medium. Work in one direction, starting from one corner and moving across systematically and evenly. Do not go back over an area that has started to crackle, as this will destroy the finish.

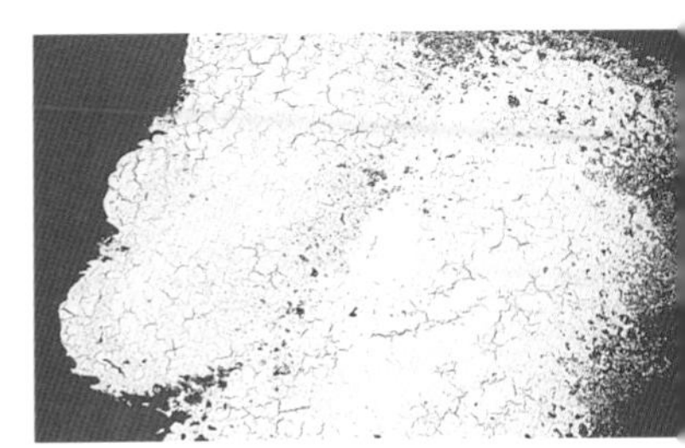

3 As the paint dries, cracks in the top coat will appear. Allow to dry for at least 24 hours, as it is best to leave a crackled surface to fully set before adding a design.

Brush crackle

This wine-cask holder has been brush crackled, and then painted over with a rich grape design.

YOU WILL NEED

- **Palette: Admiral Blue base with Dove Grey**
- **Brushes: 2 wide brushes**
- **Prepared base (see pages 26–29)**
- **Crackle medium**
- **Tinting dish**
- **Dry palette**

1 Follow step 1 of Sponge crackle (see page 37).

2 Transfer some acrylic paint to the palette and load a wide brush generously with paint. Working on one surface area at a time, brush on the top color over the dry crackle medium.

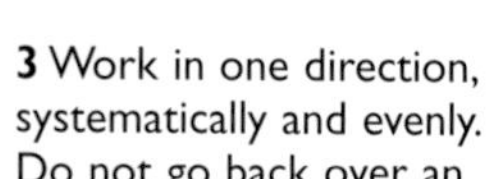

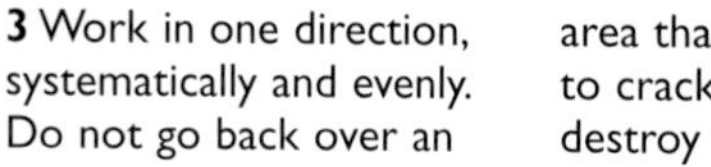

3 Work in one direction, systematically and evenly. Do not go back over an area that has started to crackle, as this will destroy the finish.

4 As the paint dries, cracks in the top coat will appear. Allow to dry for a least 24 hours.

Top crackle

Top crackle mediums are painted over the finished piece of work and are especially good for creating an aged look on a painted motif, not just on a background. The two parts of the process react with each other to create the appearance of aged varnish. Finish with a wash of Raw Umber to really show up the cracks and give a well worn-look.

YOU WILL NEED

- **Palette: Buttermilk base and Raw Umber**
- **Brushes: 3 wide brushes**
- **Prepared base (see pages 26–29), complete with painted design**
- **Two-part top crackle medium**
- **Tinting dish**
- **Wet palette**
- **Dry palette**

1 Pour a little of the first mixture of a two-part top crackle medium into a tinting dish.

RIGHT *The pollen on the stamens subtely picks up the color of the brush-crackled background.*

LEFT *The top of this bin has a brush crackle finish, effectively adding a little texture to an object that, with its four large surfaces, might otherwise appear a little "flat."*

2 Load a wide brush with crackle medium and brush it evenly over a completely dry painted surface. Leave to dry thoroughly.

3 Pour some of the second mixture into a tinting dish and paint evenly over the dry first layer.

4 As it dries, cracks will appear.

5 To accentuate the cracks, mix a very small amount of Raw Umber with water to make a thin wash, and apply. The more paint you use, the more exaggerated the effect.

LEFT This small paper doily is just the right size for a coaster box. Doilies come in all shapes and sizes and make ideal background stencils.

RIGHT A piece of tissue paper was decoupaged onto the lid of this box before it was painted over with flowers.

Stenciling

Stenciled designs are often lacking in detail, but you can use them as a background and go on to enhance them with decorative painting.

YOU WILL NEED

- **Palette: Dove Grey base with White**
- **Brushes: stippling brush or small stencil brush**
- **Prepared base (see pages 28–29)**
- **Stencil**
- **Cloth**
- **Masking tape**
- **Scissors**
- **Wet palette**
- **Dry palette**
- **Paper towel**

1 I have used a doily as a stencil. Smooth out the stencil, especially if it has been used before, by rubbing it with a cloth to completely flatten it.

2 Position the stencil on the prepared base and anchor it in place with masking tape.

3 Transfer some acrylic paint to a wet palette. Pick up a little paint on a stippling or small stencil brush and work the brush into a dry palette.

4 Dab the brush on a paper towel until most of the paint is removed.

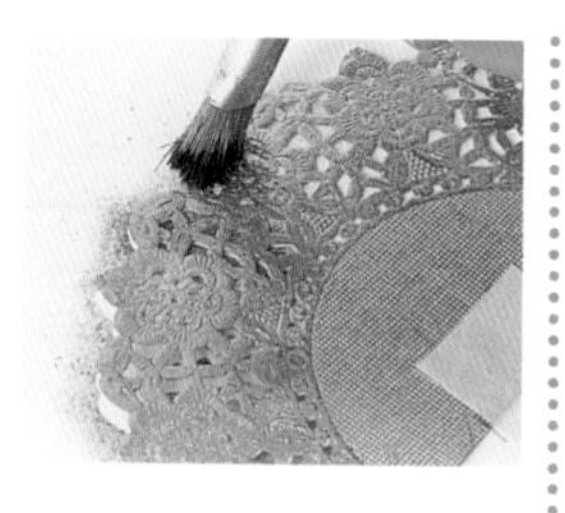

5 Hold the brush vertically and dab the bristles evenly all over the stencil, pushing the paint through the holes and onto the base.

6 Leave to dry completely before carefully peeling back the stencil. You can now add another design or embellish the stencil with decorative painting.

DON'T TRY THIS

Do not attempt to stencil on a papier-mâché object, as you will not achieve an even print.

Decoupage

Combining decoupage and decorative painting can create some very interesting effects. Choose an image on thin paper, or photocopy an old photograph. For lettering you could type a word or sentence in your favorite typeface and print it on a laser printer, or use type cut from a catalog or magazine.

YOU WILL NEED

- **Palette: Buttermilk base**
- **Brushes: 2 wide brushes**
- **Prepared base (see pages 28–29)**
- **Square cut from silk paper**
- **Sharp scissors**
- **Multipurpose sealer**

1 Carefully cut out your chosen motif. If you are using a paper napkin, only cut out the motif on the top layer.

RIGHT The early Greek-style motif was decoupaged onto the pot and enhanced with pencil cyprus trees.

2 Use a wide brush to apply a coat of multi-purpose sealer to the back of the cut motif. Leave to dry.

3 Brush a coat of multipurpose sealer onto the prepared surface and again onto the back of the motif, but do not allow it to dry. Smooth the motif onto the surface, using a clean wide brush to glide it into position, and gently brush out any air bubbles. Leave to dry.

4 Apply another layer of sealer, and allow to dry.

Cypress trees pot

Adding a pre-printed motif to a painted surface and then adding a design gives an extra dimension. Here, the classical border compliments the Mediterranean trees.

YOU WILL NEED

- **Palette: Buttermilk base with Asphaltum, Black Green, Hauser Dark Green, Hauser Light Green**
- **Brushes: 2 wide brushes, No. 1 liner, deerfoot (see pages 88–89)**
- **4-inch (10cm) terra-cotta pot, sealed and base coated (see pages 28–29)**
- **Motif printed on paper**
- **Sharp scissors**
- **Multipurpose sealer**
- **Wet palette**
- **Dry palette**
- **Paper towel**

1 Follow steps 1–4 of Decoupage to apply a paper motif to a sealed terra-cotta pot.

2 Transfer some Asphaltum paint to a wet palette. Load a liner brush and paint thin lines of varying height to define tree trunks.

3 Transfer Black Green and Hauser Dark Green to a dry palette. Load a deerfoot (see pages 88–89) with Black Green on the heel and Hauser Dark Green on the toe. Tap in the tree shapes starting from the top and working down.

4 Wipe the brush, but do not clean it, and pick up a little Hauser Light Green on the toe. Tap in the highlights at the front and right of each tree.

5 Leave for 24 hours before protecting the painted finish (see pages 114–115).

also see the following pages
Applying the base coat 28–29
Masking 32 • **Stripes** 33 • **Sponging** 32
Pivot stroke 56 • **Liner brushstrokes** 62–64
Double loading 80–82 • **Applying your finish** 114–115

Project 1

Striped CD box with ivy leaves

This simple project uses a sponged background between masking tape stripes, embellished with a two-color leaf motif. Reversing the leaf colors on the dark and light backgrounds ensures that they stand out in each case.

YOU WILL NEED

- **Palette: Buttermilk base with Hauser Dark Dreen, Hauser Light Green, Buttermilk, and Titanium White**
- **Brushes: wide flat brush, No. 1 liner, No. 10 flat brush, synthetic brush for varnishing**
- **Sealed wooden CD box (see pages 28–27)**
- **Fine-grade sandpaper**
- **Masking tape**
- **Scissors**
- **Wet palette**
- **Natural sponge**
- **Dry palette**
- **18-ct gold marker pen**
- **Spray sealer**
- **Matte varnish**

1 Use a wide flat brush to apply a Buttermilk base coat to all except the short side of the sealed CD box. Sand and repeat, then dry thoroughly.

2 Cut masking tape strips to size and press onto the base-coated sides to mask off evenly spaced, wide stripes.

3 Use a liner to paint a thin line of Buttermilk along the edge of the masking tape to further seal the edge and prevent any leakage of the top color. Leave to dry.

4 Transfer small amounts of paint to a wet palette. Use a wide brush to paint the stripes and the short side of the box with Hauser Dark Green. Allow to dry and repeat.

The high end of the box has a light background, with dark-edged leaves.

5 Moisten a natural sponge and use it to pick up a little Hauser Light Green.

6 Dab the sponge into the dry palette to work the paint evenly through it.

7 Press the sponge evenly over the dry painted stripes. Reload with paint as necessary and change the sponge when it becomes saturated with paint. Leave to dry.

10 Double load a No. 10 flat brush with Hauser Dark Green and Hauser Light Green and blend on the dry palette. Paint in the leaves freehand with the dark green on the outer side of the leaves. Start with the central leaf, working two pivot strokes back-to-back. Add two single leaves starting at the same point. Arrange the leaf formations evenly across the surface and reload the brush frequently.

8 Use a clean sponge to sparingly sponge on Buttermilk over the previously sponged stripes.

9 When all the paintwork is completely dry, carefully peel off the masking tape.

11 With the same brush, paint the leaves on the front of the box, this time keeping the light green to the outer edge.

12 Mix Hauser Dark and Light Green together, and thin to the consistency of ink. Using a clean liner, paint in curvy lines to join the leaves together and add some extra tendrils. Also pull a curved vein down the center of each leaf. Leave to dry.

13 Thin some Titanium White to the consistency of ink and, with a clean liner, add a small highlight line to the middle of each vein. Allow to dry.

14 Use an 18-ct gold marker pen to run a gold edge around the top of the box. Let dry.

15 Apply a light spray of sealer. Leave for 24 hours and finish with several coats of matte varnish.

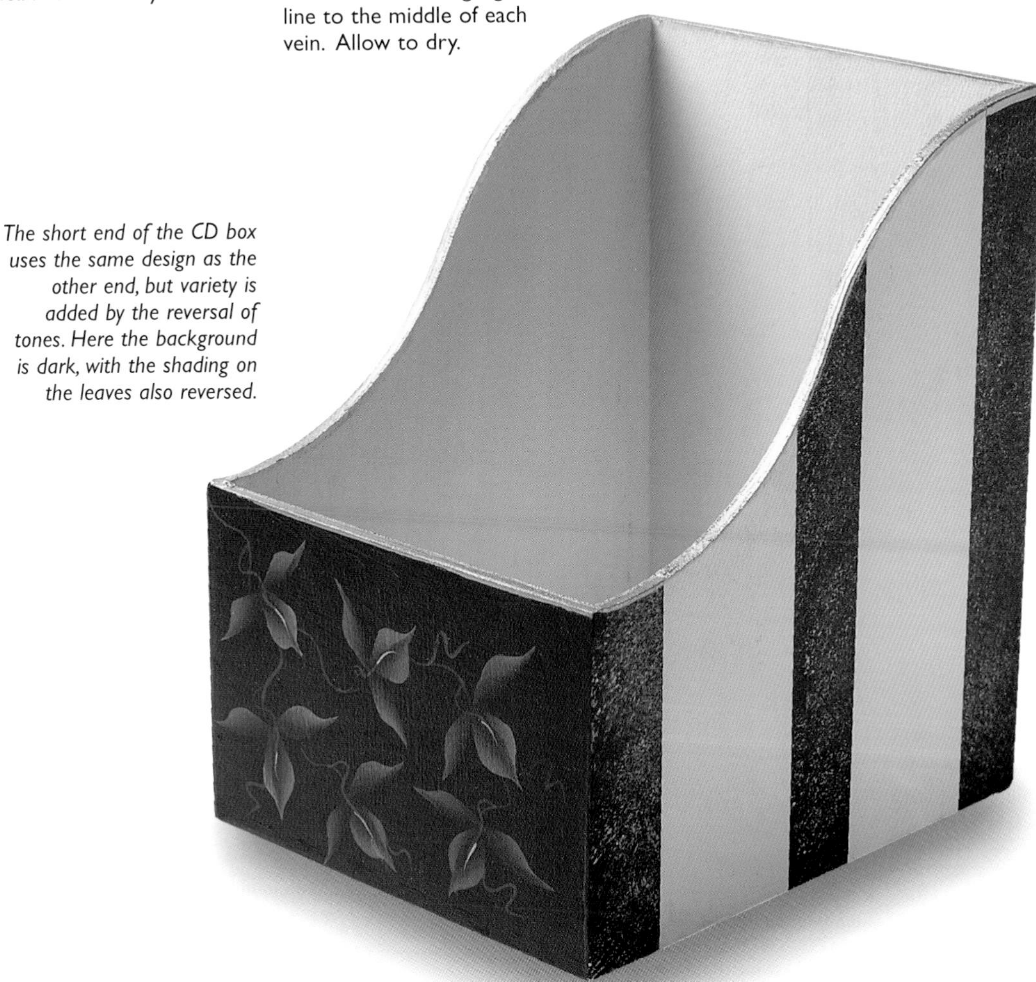

The short end of the CD box uses the same design as the other end, but variety is added by the reversal of tones. Here the background is dark, with the shading on the leaves also reversed.

ESSENTIAL STROKES

ESSENTIAL STROKES

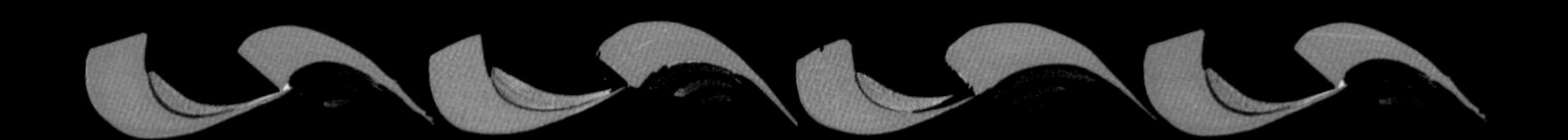

Simple and easy to execute, even on their own these strokes can form lovely motifs and borders. Many of the more complicated techniques rely on these strokes, so it is important to be comfortable with them before moving on.

Brush loading and brushwork basics

You have chosen, prepared, and base coated your surface, and have perhaps even applied a background paint effect. Sitting comfortably at your workspace with brush in hand, it is now time for the fun part.

These bright red pansies are painted with ruffled pivot strokes (see pages 56–58).

YOU WILL NEED

- **Palette: Cadmium Yellow**
- **Brushes: round brush, flat brush**
- **Tinting dish**
- **Easi Float retarder**
- **Paper towel**
- **Dry palette**

1 Pour about 2 tsp (10ml) of clean water into a tinting dish.

2 Add two or three drops of retarder to the water. This is the retarder mix, used to aid the flow of the paint.

3 Moisten your round brush in the retarder mix. With the exception of certain dry-brush strokes (see page 49), you should always moisten your brush before loading it with acrylic paint.

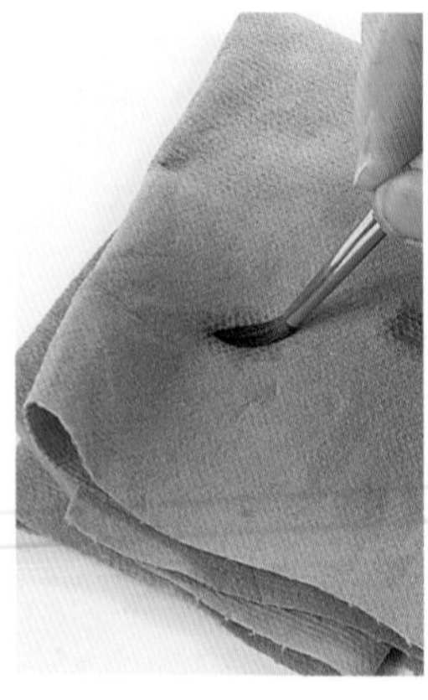

4 Pat the brush on a paper towel to remove the excess retarder mix.

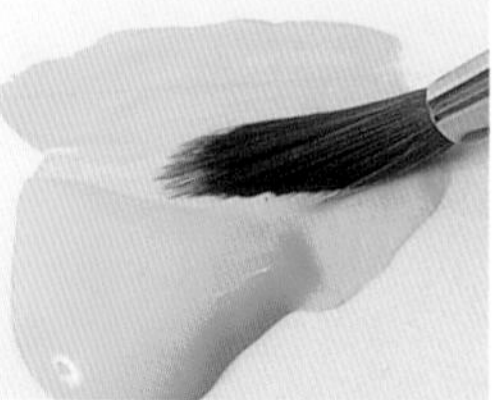

5 Transfer some acrylic paint to a dry palette. Dip the moistened brush into the puddle of paint.

6 Smooth the paint into the brush so that it is no more than two-thirds of the way up the bristles. Repeat until the brush is full of paint.

7 Gently roll the bristles on the dry palette to reshape the brush.

8 Load a flat brush in the same way, but to reshape it, press down onto the palette.

But first things first. To achieve good strokes you need to have your brush properly loaded. An overloaded brush will result in thick lines of paint down the outer sides of your strokes. If you load too little paint, there will not be sufficient to complete the stroke. Follow these steps and you will soon be loading your brush perfectly.

This tray uses fairly basic strokework, mainly double-loaded commas, to create an elaborate design.

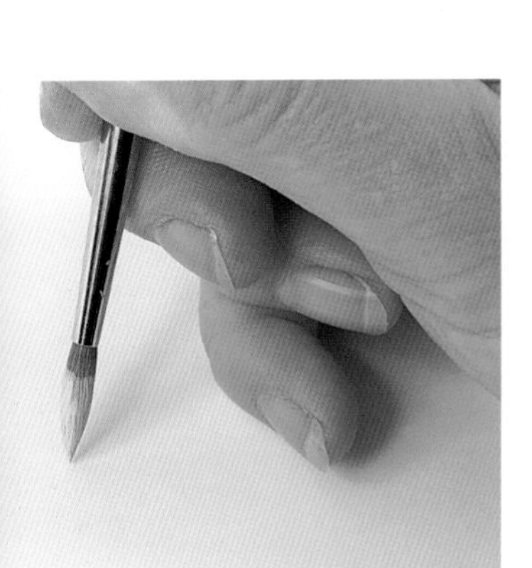

9 When painting, support your hand by resting on your curled little finger. In this position you will be able to move your brush freely without using your shoulder. Always work toward you. If you push the brush away from you, the bristles will spread, and you will lose control of the stroke.

10 Always rinse your brush before changing paint colors, so as to obtain a clean color each time.

Basic brush loading kit

Your basic brush loading kit, necessary for most of the techniques and projects in this book, will consist of a brush basin, a retarder mix in a tinting dish, a wet palette, and a dry palette.

Dry brushing

The texture of dry brushing depends on the type of brush you use. A soft round brush will give a softer effect than a course stippling brush.

YOU WILL NEED

- **Palette: Antique Teal**
- **Brushes: round brush**
- **Paper towel**
- **Dry palette**

1 Take a dry brush and dip the tip in the paint.

2 Work the paint into the brush on a dry palette.

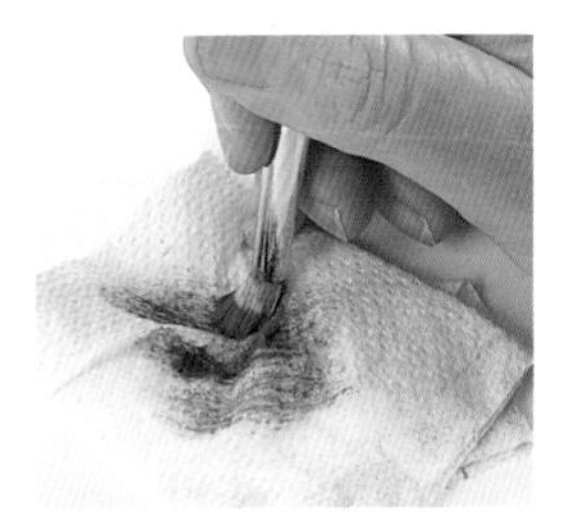

3 Brush onto a paper towel to remove excess paint. The paint on the brush should be barely visible.

4 Apply to the surface. Re-apply to build up the desired amount of color.

Round brushstrokes

Round brushstrokes are the basis for a large number of folk-art styles. Barge or canal boat painting uses simple commas in primary colors to create its distinctive designs. More sophisticated folk-art forms use similar strokes loaded with two or more colors. A round brush is traditionally used for the extravagant Russian-style painting, called "Zhostovo," in which several thin layers of paint build up flower and leaf shapes.

This pretty box uses round- and flat-brush strokework, with floated shading and highlighting.

Straight comma

YOU WILL NEED

- **Palette: Country Red**
- **Brushes: round brush**
- **Basic brush loading kit (see page 49)**

1 Load a round brush with paint. Press the tip of the brush down on the dry palette to flatten the end slightly.

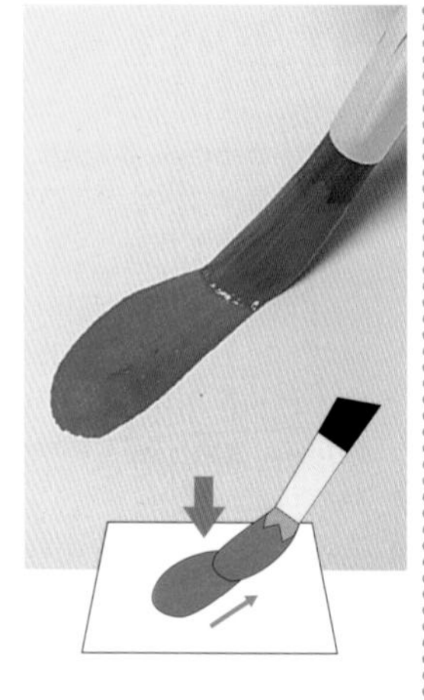

3 Keeping the line straight, pull slowly toward you, gradually raising the brush and letting it come back to a point.

2 Hold the brush upright and press it down on the surface to be painted to spread the bristles.

4 Lift the brush off the surface.

Curved comma

YOU WILL NEED

- **Palette: Country Red**
- **Brushes: round brush**
- **Basic brush loading kit (see page 49)**

1 Repeat steps 1–2 of Straight comma.

2 Curve the line into a gentle arc as you slowly pull it toward you, gradually raising the brush and letting it come back to a point.

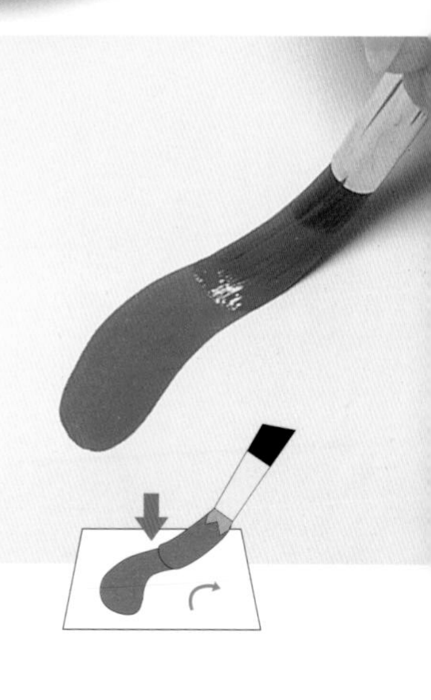

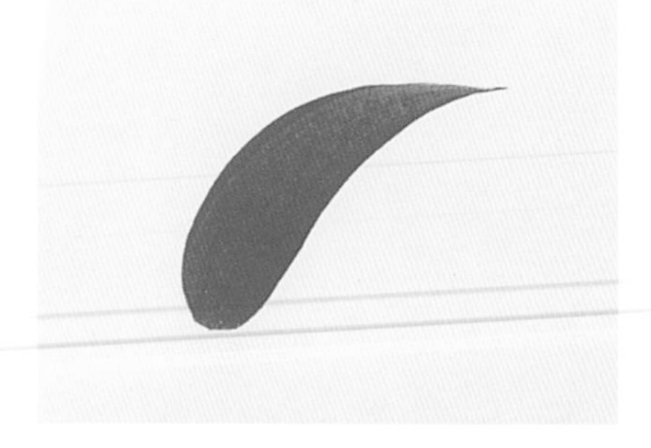

3 Lift the brush off the surface.

KEY → *Direction of brush*  *Heavy pressure*  *Medium pressure* ↓ *Light pressure*

Curved commas are ideal for flowers and leaves. Used in groups they can form a simple stand-alone motif, and as part of a larger design they can form a fill-in flower or spray of leaves without detracting from the main focal point.

Mastery of round brushstrokes is the key to brush control, and it is well worth taking time to practice each type of stroke until it becomes second nature. Remember that the more pressure you apply to the brush, the wider it will spread and the broader your

Napkin box with comma daisies and double-loaded leaves.

Round-brush comma daisy

Of all the flowers you will paint as a folk artist, daisies are the most popular, particularly white ones. A simple monochrome motif on a dark background will look very striking without any further enhancement.

YOU WILL NEED

- **Palette: Hauser Dark Green base, with Titanium White, Golden Straw, Terra Cotta, and Hauser Medium Green**
- **Brushes: No. 3 or 5 round brush**
- **Basic brush loading kit (see page 49)**
- **Motif, tracing paper, masking tape, transfer paper, and stylus (optional)**

1 Either paint freehand or transfer a design to the prepared and base-coated surface (see page 25).

2 Load a round brush with Titanium White and press the tip down on the dry palette to flatten the end slightly.

3 Paint curved commas to fill in all the petals. Allow to dry.

4 Rinse the brush. Pick up some Golden Straw and paint in the center with two straight commas. Leave to dry.

5 Rinse the brush and side load with Terra Cotta (see page 66). Shade the bottom of the flower center. Leave to dry.

6 Rinse and dry the brush thoroughly. Use a dry brush to highlight the top of the center with a very little Titanium White (see page 106).

7 Rinse the brush and load as usual with thinned Hauser Medium Green. Paint in the stalk using just the tip of the brush.

8 Paint in the remaining petals.

stroke will be. The length and thickness of the tail on a comma stroke depends on the amount of pressure applied as you move the brush toward you and onto its tip. Pay attention to the way you hold the brush and pull the stroke toward you, and you will soon produce a consistent result.

Practicing comma strokes is also a very good way of getting your hand moving smoothly and confidently before you start painting a design.

Ribbon

YOU WILL NEED

- **Palette: Deep Burgundy**
- **Brushes: round brush**
- **Basic brush loading kit (see page 49)**

1 Load a round brush with paint and press the tip down on the dry palette to flatten the end slightly.

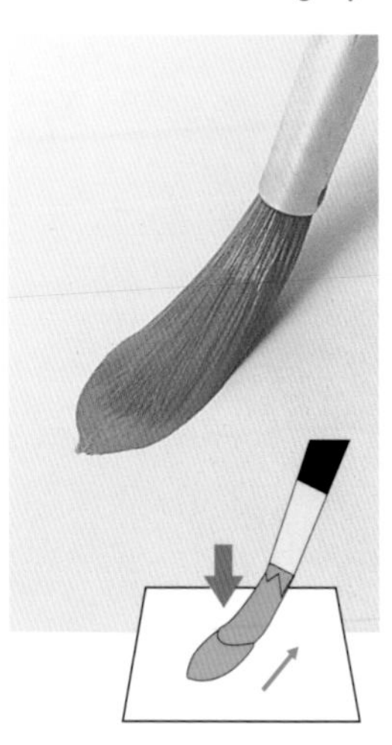

2 Hold the brush upright and press it down on the surface to be painted to spread the bristles.

3 Gently pull the brush toward you, gradually increasing the pressure in the center of the stroke, and then release it to give an even shape, ending on the tip of the bristles.

4 Starting next to the previous stroke and overlapping it slightly, repeat steps 2–3 to build up a long ribbon.

Ribbon and comma bow

YOU WILL NEED

- **Palette: Admiral Blue base with Titanium White**
- **Brushes: No. 3 or 5 round brush**
- **Basic brush loading kit (see page 49)**
- **Motif, tracing paper, masking tape, transfer paper, and stylus (optional)**

1 Either paint freehand or transfer a design to the prepared and base-coated surface (see page 25).

2 Load a round brush with Titanium White and press the tip down on the dry palette to flatten the end slightly.

KEY → *Direction of brush*  *Heavy pressure* *Medium pressure* *Light pressure*

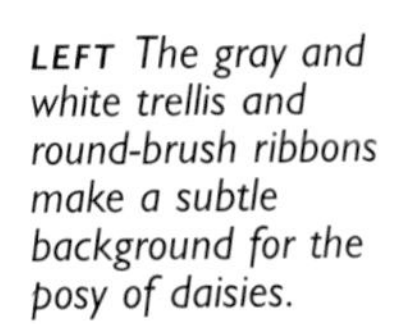

LEFT The gray and white trellis and round-brush ribbons make a subtle background for the posy of daisies.

RIGHT A few simple white comma strokes against a dark blue background have transformed a very simple papier-mâché item into a special gift or trinket box.

3 Paint a straight comma (see page 50) for the knot of the bow.

4 Pull two curved ribbon strokes out from the top two corners of the knot and two slightly longer ones down from the bottom corners.

5 Join up each pair of ribbons with a curved comma.

6 Add a ribbon stroke either side of the knot, traveling vertically down, to start the bow's tails.

7 Finish with a curved comma stroke on each tail, traveling outward.

Flat brushstrokes

The flat brush is my favorite brush because it is so adaptable. Its chisel edge is useful for painting very fine lines, and broad stripes can be produced by simply pressing it down. Turning it by degrees, you can make the most of both these attributes.

A good flat brush has a fine chisel edge, and the brush should be held almost upright

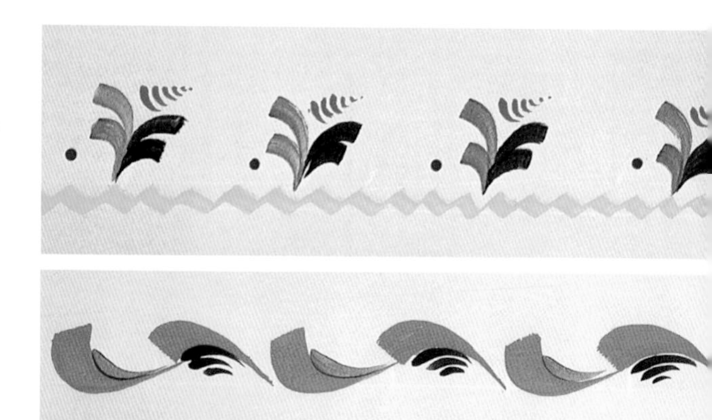

Broad stroke

YOU WILL NEED

- **Palette: Hauser Dark Green**
- **Brushes: flat brush**
- **Basic brush loading kit (see page 49)**

1 Load a flat brush by pulling it through the edge of a puddle of paint, then turn it over and repeat on the other side.

2 Blend on a dry palette to distribute the paint evenly through the brush. The paint should not travel more than two-thirds of the way up the bristles.

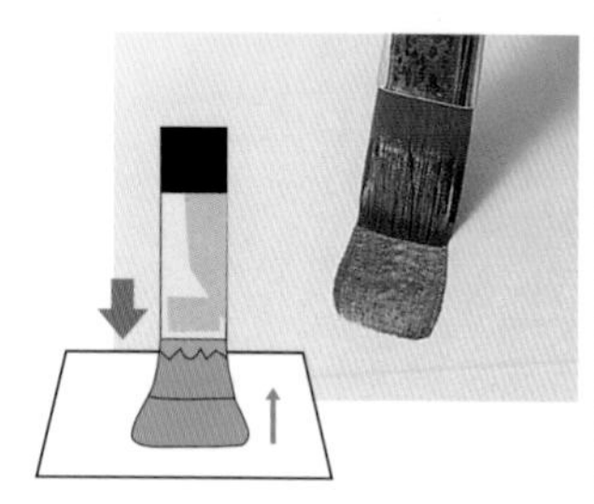

3 Hold the brush upright and touch the chisel edge on the surface to be painted. Pull the brush toward you to paint a broad flat stroke. Lift off.

Straight comma

YOU WILL NEED

- **Palette: Deep Burgundy**
- **Brushes: flat brush**
- **Basic brush loading kit (see page 49)**

1 Repeat steps 1–2 of Broad stroke.

2 Hold the brush upright and touch the chisel edge on the surface to be painted. Press down gradually, bringing the brush toward you.

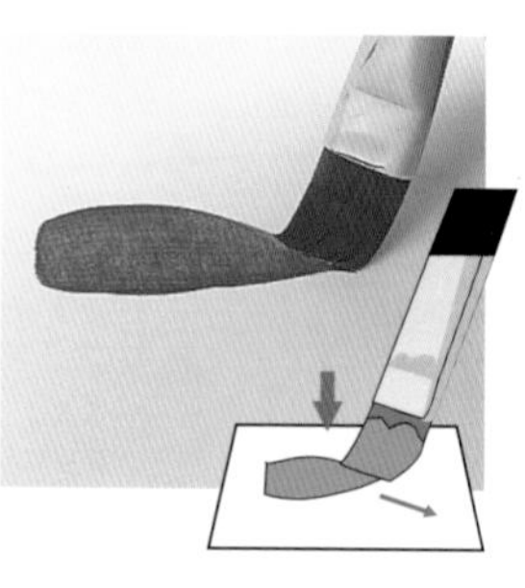

3 Still bringing the brush toward you, turn it through 90°, releasing the pressure. End on the chisel edge and lift off.

Curved comma

YOU WILL NEED

- **Palette: Deep Burgundy**
- **Brushes: flat brush**
- **Basic brush loading kit (see page 49)**

1 Repeat steps 1–2 of broad flat stroke.

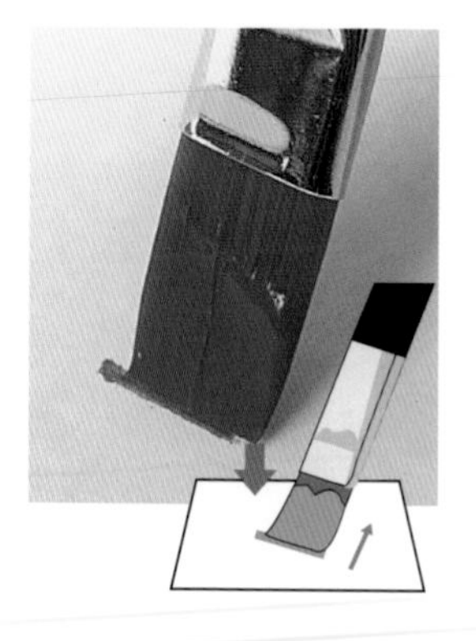

2 Hold the brush upright and touch the chisel edge on the surface to be painted. Press down gradually, curving the stroke in an arc toward you.

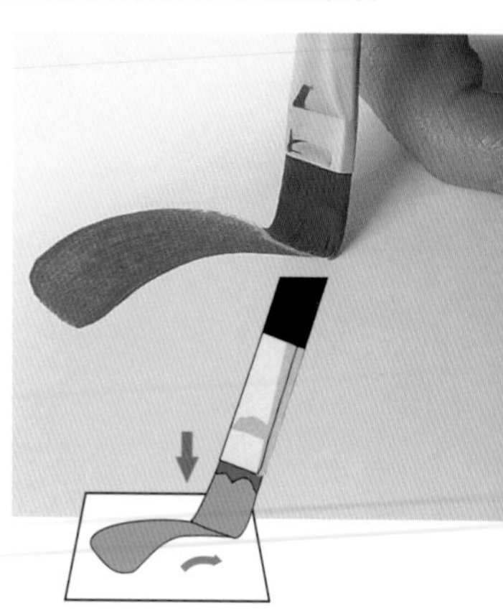

3 Releasing the pressure, turn the brush through 90°. End on the chisel edge and lift off.

KEY 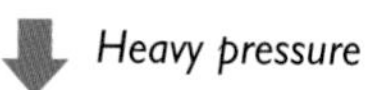 *Direction of brush* *Heavy pressure* *Medium pressure* *Light pressure*

RIGHT *A group of flat-brush commas and linerwork make up this simple iris design on a small gift box.*

LEFT *Flat-brush and round-brush commas come together to create a structured border.*

Flat-brush comma iris

YOU WILL NEED

- **Palette: French Grey-Blue base with Black Plum, Golden Straw, Titanium White, Hauser Medium Green**
- **Brushes: No. 8 or 10 flat brush, No. 1 liner**
- **Basic brush loading kit (see page 49)**
- **Motif, tracing paper, masking tape, transfer paper, and stylus or empty ballpoint pen (optional)**

1 Either paint freehand or transfer a design to the prepared and base-coated surface (see page 25).

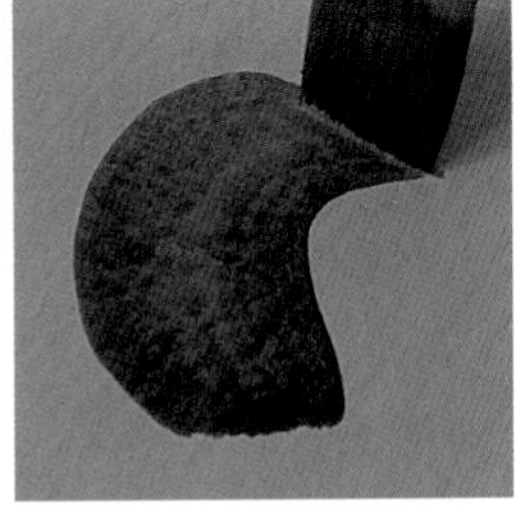

2 Load a flat brush with Black Plum and pull in a curved comma from the side to what will be the center of the flower. Repeat on the other side. These two comma strokes can be ruffled to give variety (see page 58).

3 Reload the brush and pull down a straight comma to meet the two curved commas.

4 Turn the work around. Load the rinsed brush with Golden Straw and pull a straight comma into the center.

5 Add the details with a liner (see page 62–65), using Black Plum for the veins on the "tongue."

6 Use the liner and Titanium White to paint the veins on the dark petals. Finish the flower with a liner brush comma across the center.

7 Add the stalk with a liner and Hauser Medium Green.

to make the most of this. Flat brushes are available in different lengths. Those with a length shorter than their width are known as blenders, and the longer ones are shaders.

Like the round brush, the flat brush can be used for a wide range of strokes. It performs well with everything from leaves to letters, and once you have mastered the simpler strokes you will be able to create quite sophisticated combinations.

Chisel stroke

YOU WILL NEED

- **Palette: Asphaltum**
- **Brushes: flat brush**
- **Basic brush loading kit (see page 49)**

1 Load a flat brush by pulling it through the edge of a puddle of paint, then turn it over and repeat on the other side.

2 Blend on a dry palette to distribute the paint evenly through the brush. The paint should not travel more than two-thirds of the way up the bristles.

3 Hold the brush upright and lightly touch the chisel edge onto the surface.

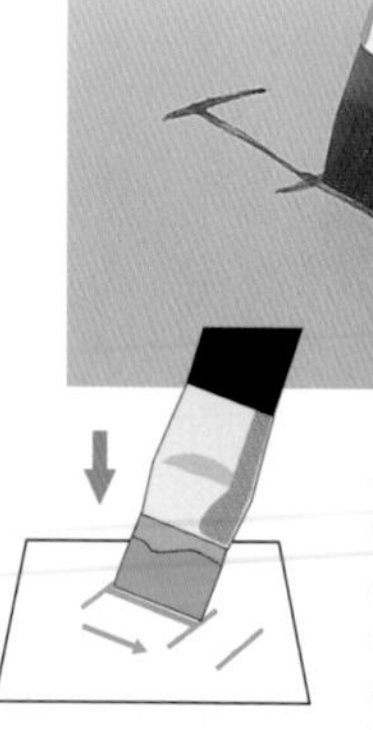

4 Apply a gentle pressure to spread the bristles just a little. Pull the brush toward you, still on its chisel edge, to paint a long, fine line.

Pivot stroke

YOU WILL NEED

- **Palette: Pansy Lavender**
- **Brushes: flat brush**
- **Basic brush loading kit (see page 49)**

1 Repeat steps 1–2 of Chisel stroke.

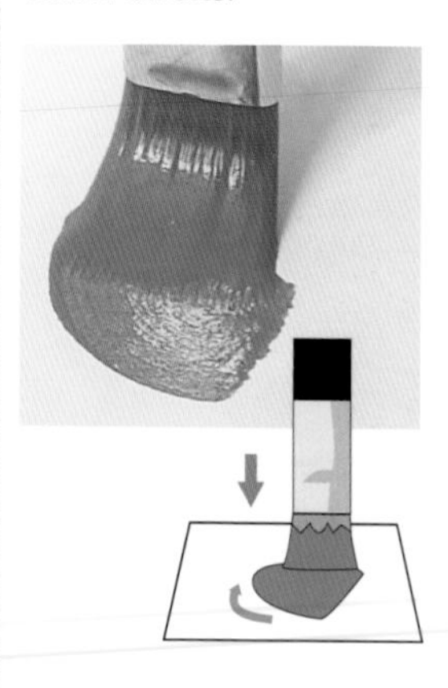

2 Hold the brush upright and touch the chisel edge to the surface. Press down a little as you pull the brush toward you.

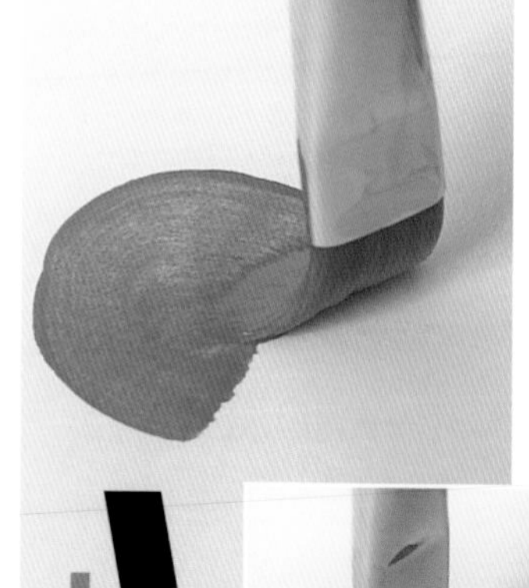

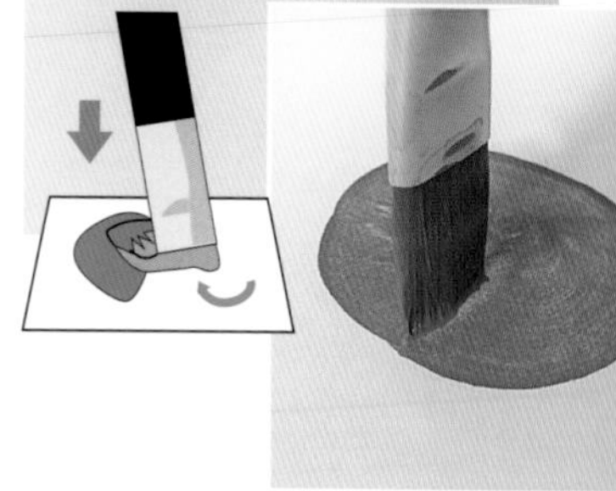

3 Keep the top corner of the brush still, and turn the brush through 360°, a full circle. Lift off.

KEY  *Direction of brush*   *Heavy pressure* 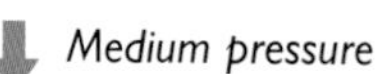 *Medium pressure* 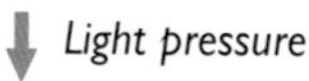 *Light pressure*

LEFT *A round-brush rooster with a chisel-stroke fence decorates the side of this utensil holder.*

RIGHT *These pivot-stroke grapes demonstrate how decorative motifs can often be created out of a couple of very simple strokes.*

Pivot-stroke grapes

YOU WILL NEED

- **Palette: Dove Grey base with Black Plum, Raw Umber, and Titanium White**
- **Brushes: No. 8 or 10 flat brush, No. 1 liner**
- **Basic brush loading kit (see page 49)**
- **Motif, tracing paper, masking tape, transfer paper, and stylus (optional)**

1 Either paint freehand or transfer a design to the prepared and base-coated surface (see page 25).

2 Load a flat brush with Black Plum, blend in the color on a dry palette, and paint in the first black grape using a pivot stroke.

3 Use the same stroke to paint more grapes of varying sizes, in a bunch.

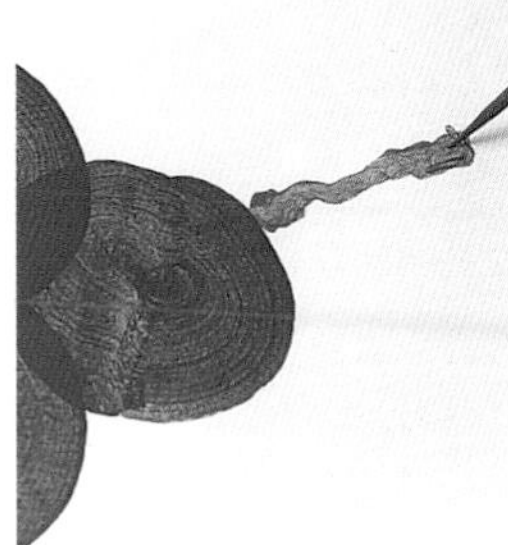

4 Add the details with a liner and Raw Umber (see pages 62–65). Wiggle the brush slightly to get a knobbly appearance.

5 Load a liner brush with Raw Umber (see pages 62–65), and paint in the fine tendrils.

6 Rinse the liner, load with Titanium White, and add small highlights to the upper right-hand side of each grape.

These double-loaded roses are formed with ruffled crescents, and sit against a sponge crackle background.

Crescent

YOU WILL NEED

- **Palette: Admiral Blue**
- **Brushes: flat brush**
- **Basic brush loading kit (see page 49)**

1 Load a flat brush by pulling it through the edge of a puddle of paint on the wet palette, then turn it over and repeat on the other side.

2 Blend on a dry palette to distribute the paint evenly through the brush. The paint should not travel more than two-thirds of the way up the bristles.

3 Imagine an arc, like an upside-down "U." Hold the brush upright with the chisel edge touching the surface at the bottom left of the imaginary arc, or the bottom right if you are left-handed. Move the brush upward and outward in a curved line.

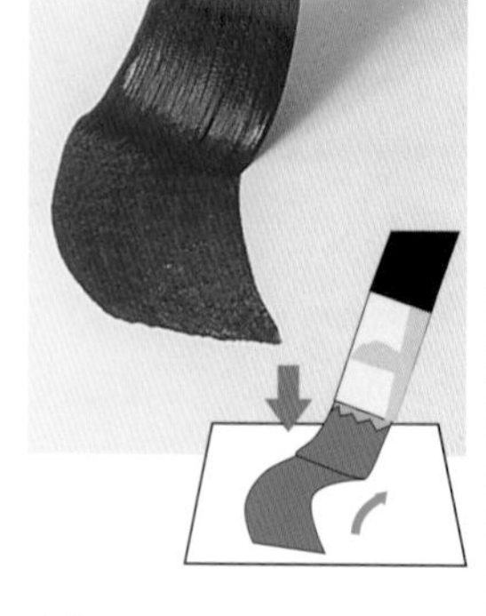

4 Keep moving the brush upward, gradually adding pressure and keeping the lower side of the brush on the imaginary arc line.

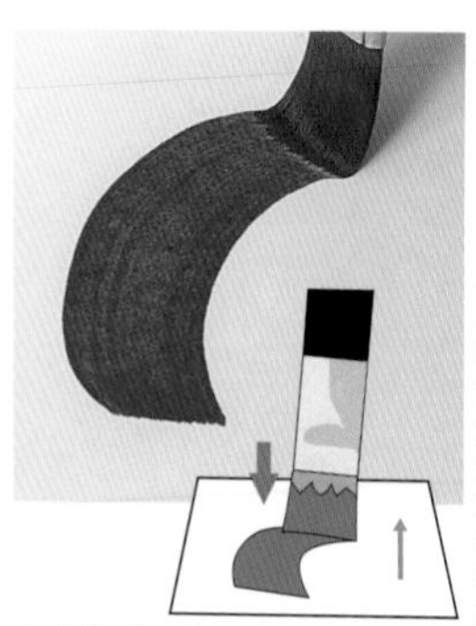

5 Pull the brush across the top of the arc, gradually, so you end the stroke on the chisel edge again. Lift off. Practice this stroke until you achieve a symmetrical crescent.

Ruffled crescent

YOU WILL NEED

- **Palette: Admiral Blue**
- **Brushes: flat brush**
- **Basic brush loading kit (see page 49)**

1 Repeat steps 1–3 of Crescent stroke.

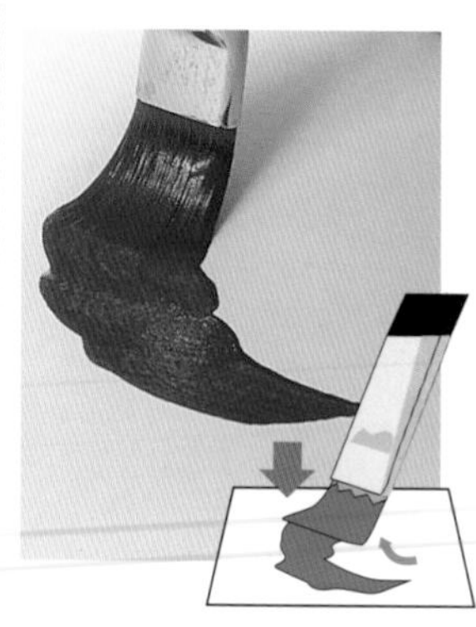

2 As you pull the brush across the arc, press it into small curves.

3 Release the pressure as you pull the brush back into the line of the arc, finishing on the chisel edge. Lift off.

KEY  *Direction of brush* *Heavy pressure* 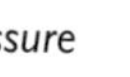 *Medium pressure* *Light pressure*

The fine ruffles on the rose petals give them a soft, natural appearance.

The gold edge nicely finishes this coaster, with its simple crescent-stroke tulip.

Crescent tulip

YOU WILL NEED

- **Palette: Dove Grey base with Raspberry, Antique Teal, and Black Plum**
- **Brushes: No. 10 flat brush, No. 2 round brush**
- **Basic brush loading kit (see page 49)**
- **Motif, tracing paper, masking tape, transfer paper, and stylus (optional)**

1 Either paint freehand or transfer the design to the prepared and base-coated surface (see page 25).

2 Load a flat brush with Antique Teal and paint ruffled strokes, like the ruffled crescent, but working in a diagonal line like elongated commas (see page 54). Finish on the chisel edge as usual, but flick the stroke up.

3 Use the same stroke, varying the lengths and frequency of ruffles, to complete all the leaves.

4 Use Antique Teal and a pivot stroke (see page 56) to paint in the stalk.

5 Rinse the brush and load with Raspberry. Paint an upside down crescent, ending one side higher than the other, for the flower.

6 Load a round brush with Black Plum, and add three tiny straight commas for the stamens (see page 50).

7 Rinse the round brush and load with Antique Teal. Pull two curved commas out from the base of the flower.

"S" and "Z" strokes

"S" and "Z" strokes can be executed with a flat, round, or liner brush. One "S" stroke can be a petal or leaf, and used in groups they can form tiny fill-in sprays or a major element of a design. The "S" stands for "slide." The "Z" stroke is commonly used in brush lettering, and also looks good in groups. A line of "Z" strokes makes a decorative zigzag border.

"S" stroke

YOU WILL NEED

- **Palette: Cadmium Orange**
- **Brushes: flat brush**
- **Basic brush loading kit (see page 49)**

1 Load a flat brush by pulling it through the edge of a puddle of paint, then turn it over and repeat on the other side.

2 Blend on a dry palette to distribute the paint evenly through the brush. The paint should not travel more than two-thirds of the way up the bristles.

3 Hold the brush upright and touch the chisel edge on the surface to be painted. Start to slide the brush toward you without pressing down.

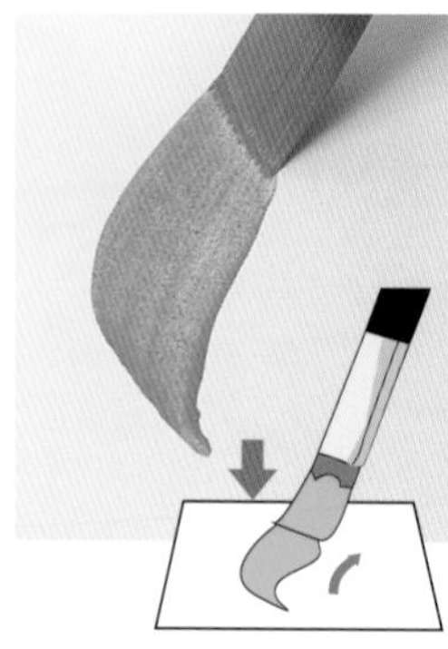

4 As you begin to press down, bring the brush toward you diagonally. The more you press the wider the stroke will be.

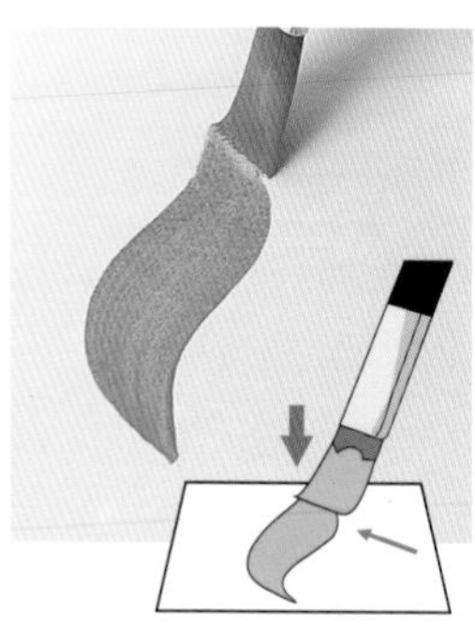

5 Gradually release the pressure as you change the direction of the brush to form a tail opposite the starting point (like a fat "S") and end on the chisel edge. Lift off.

"S"-stroke ribbon

YOU WILL NEED

- **Palette: Cadmium Orange**
- **Brushes: flat brush**
- **Basic brush loading kit (see page 49)**

1 To paint a ribbon with the flat brush, start with an elongated "S" stroke.

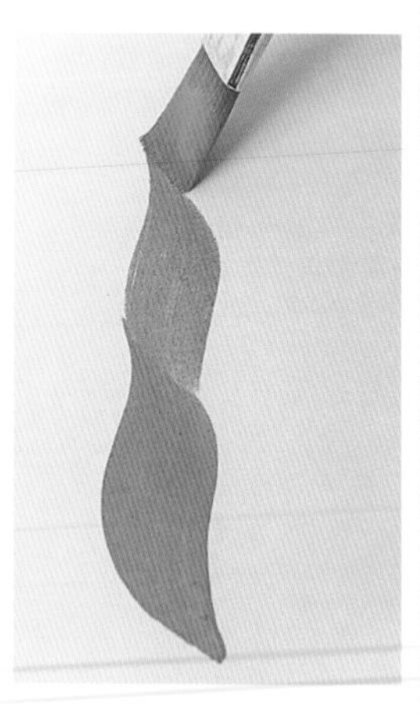

2 Paint another elongated "S" next to and slightly overlapping the first. Continue until the ribbon is the desired length.

"Z" stroke

YOU WILL NEED

- **Palette: Cadmium Orange**
- **Brushes: flat brush**
- **Basic brush loading kit (see page 49)**

1 Repeat steps 1–2 of the "S" stroke.

2 Touching the chisel edge to the surface, slide the brush sideways a little.

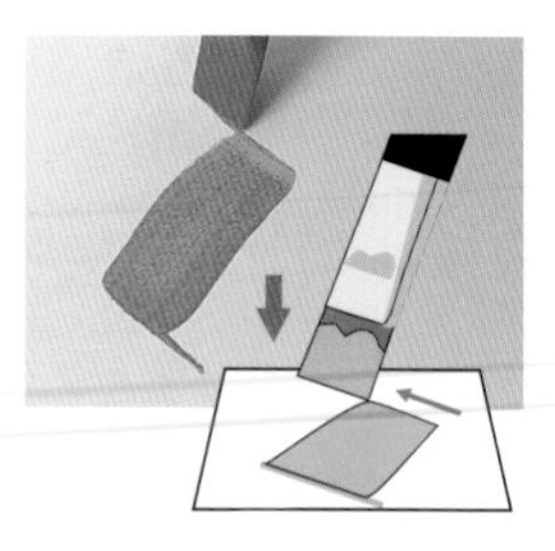

3 Lightly pull the brush toward you, then move the brush to the side on the chisel edge.

KEY → *Direction of brush*  *Heavy pressure*  *Medium pressure* *Light pressure*

LEFT The border of this perpetual calendar features a different plant for each month. The letters and numbers are painted with flat-brush "S" and "Z" strokes.

RIGHT "S" and "Z" strokes are used in the lettering, but a very subtle use of the "S" stroke can also be seen in the green leaves.

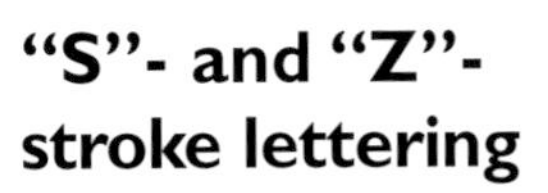

"S"- and "Z"-stroke lettering

A simple initial decorated with leaves would make a personal decoration for a card. This project would also make a pretty monogram for a special notebook or, in fabric paint, could decorate a hand towel or pillowcase.

YOU WILL NEED

- **Palette: Hauser Dark Green base with Titanium White, Hauser Medium Green, and Hauser Light Green**
- **Brushes: No. 8 flat brush, No. 1 liner, No. 2 round brush**
- **Basic brush loading kit (see page 49)**
- **Motif, tracing paper, masking tape, transfer paper, and stylus (optional)**

1 Either paint freehand or transfer a design to the prepared and base-coated surface (see page 25).

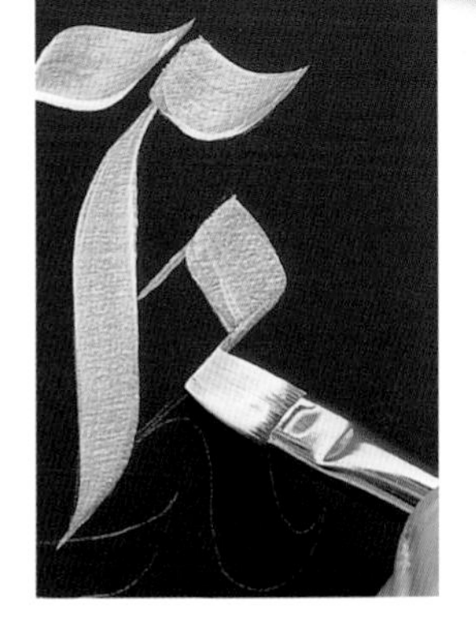

2 Load a flat brush with Titanium White and use "S" and "Z" strokes to paint in the letter, using one stroke for each element and the chisel edge for thin, straight lines (see page 56). Here, two "S" strokes form the top of a letter K. An elongated "S" forms the backbone of the letter and a variation of the basic "Z" stroke brings the finishing chisel edge line back into the letter. More "S" strokes form the "kick" of the K and the base.

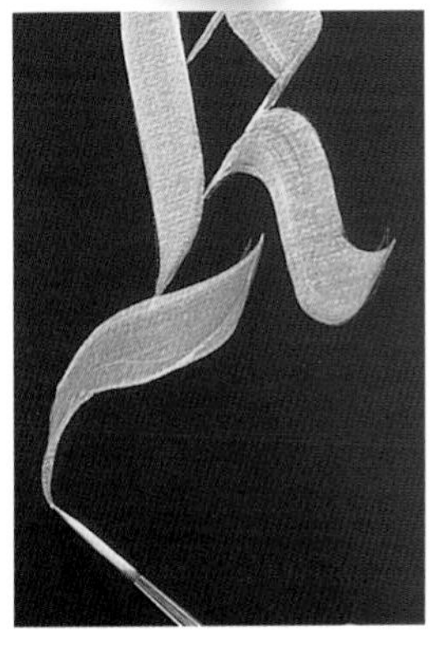

3 Load a liner with Titanium White (see pages 62–65), and use this to add the scroll ends. Let dry.

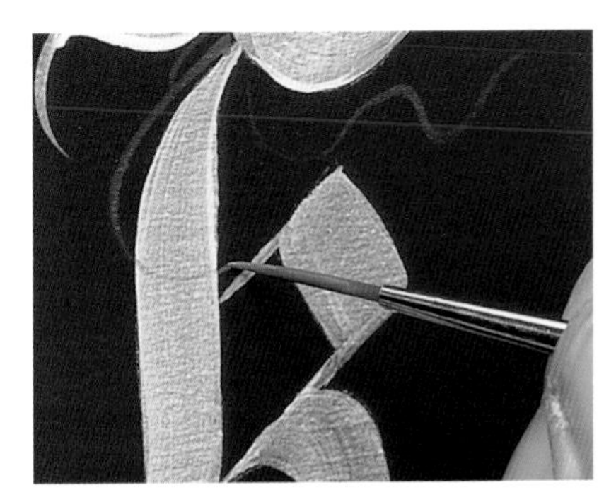

4 Rinse the liner and load with Hauser Medium Green. Weave fine lines through the structure of the letter.

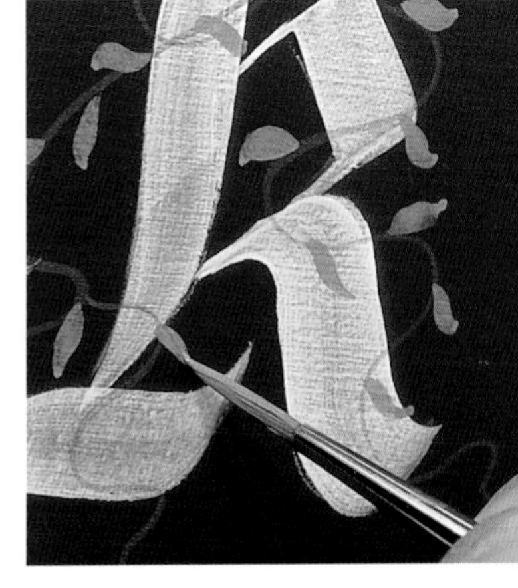

5 Load a round brush with Hauser Light Green and paint tiny commas for leaves emanating from the fine lines.

Liner brushstrokes

A liner is a fine round brush with a very sharp point, making it the perfect brush for drawing fine lines, for writing, and for intricate decoration.

Liners are available in various lengths. The longer the brush the more paint it holds, as the round part

Fine lines

YOU WILL NEED

- **Palette: Violet Haze**
- **Brushes: No. I liner**
- **Basic brush loading kit (page 49)**

1 Place paint on a wet palette and load the moistened liner brush by pulling it through the puddle of thinned paint several times.

2 Blend on the dry palette to distribute the paint evenly through the brush. The paint should not travel more than two-thirds of the way up the bristles.

3 Roll the brush as you pull it through the paint so that it retains its shape. You should be able to see the paint on the brush, but it should not be overloaded.

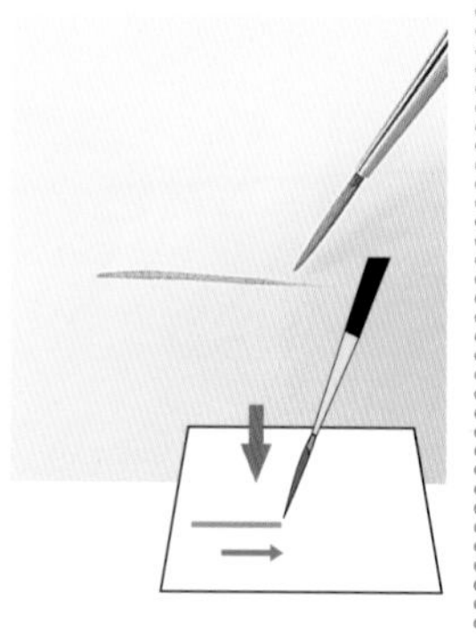

4 Hold the brush vertically over the surface to be painted and gradually lower it until the tip just touches the surface. Draw the brush toward you to form a straight stroke.

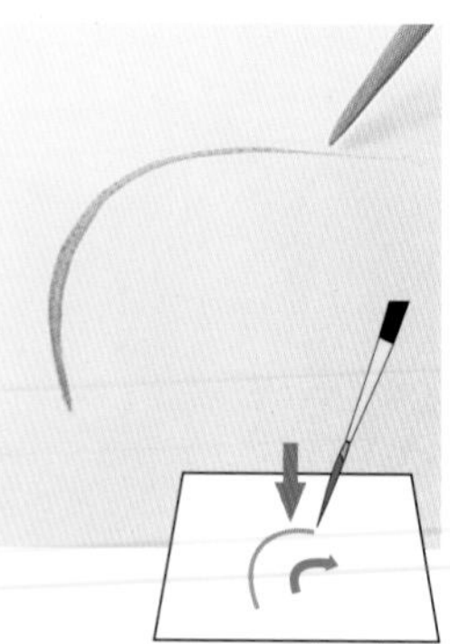

5 Pull the brush around toward you to paint a curved line.

Lace effect

YOU WILL NEED

- **Palette: Lamp Black with Metallics Pewter plastic-wrapped base, with Titanium White**
- **Brushes: No. I liner**
- **White pencil**
- **Ruler**
- **Basic brush loading kit (page 49)**
- **Stylus**

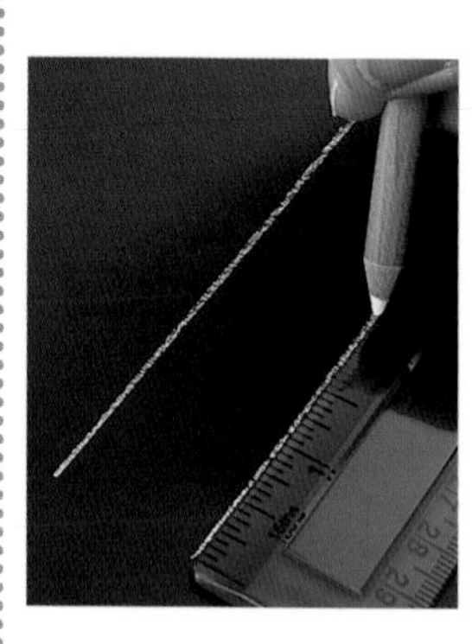

1 Using a white pencil and a ruler, lightly draw two lines marking the top and bottom of the border.

2 Mark equal intervals, approximately 1 inch (2.5cm), along the top line. Mark the same intervals along the bottom line, but start in the center of a space marked on the top line.

3 Transfer some thinned paint to a dry palette, and load a moistened liner by pulling it through the edge of the puddle of paint.

4 Blend on the dry palette to distribute the paint evenly through the brush. The paint should not travel more than two-thirds of the way up the bristles.

KEY 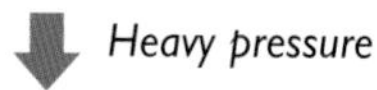 *Direction of brush* *Heavy pressure* *Medium pressure* 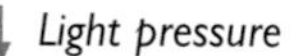 *Light pressure*

LEFT Strokework heart with a linerwork lace border.

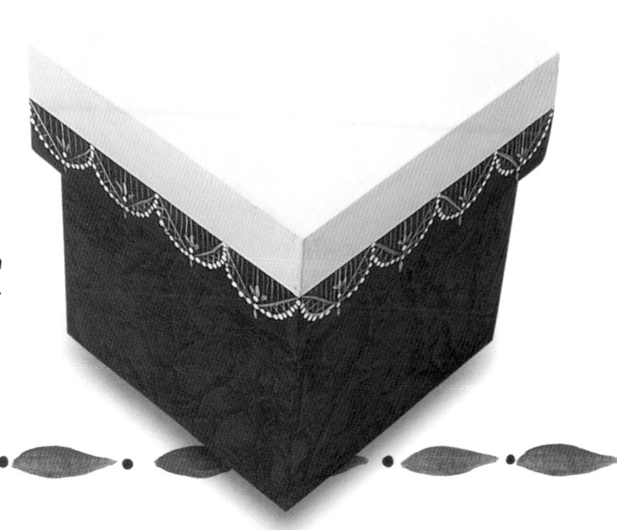

RIGHT The fine white lace effect around the rim stands out beautifully against the dark background.

5 On the dry palette, roll the brush as you pull it through the puddle so that it retains its shape. You should be able to see the paint on the brush, but it should not be overloaded.

6 Starting at one of the marks on the top line, pull a thin, straight stroke diagonally to the next bottom line mark. Continue to paint diagonal lines along the whole border.

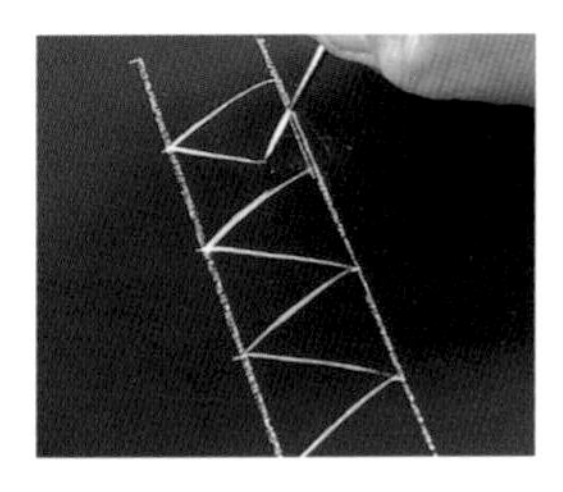

7 Paint diagonal lines in the opposite direction to form a row of triangles.

8 From the center of each triangle, pull a straight line down, then fill in with diagonal lines on either side. Repeat with all the triangles.

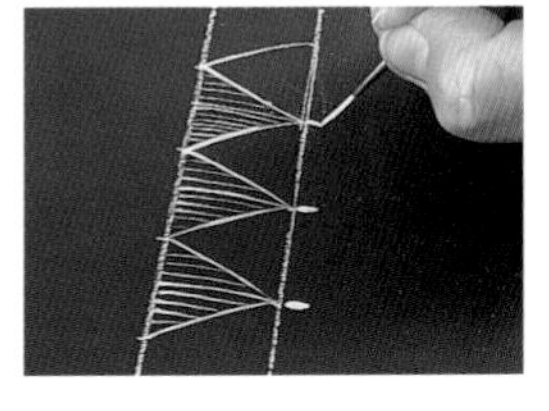

9 Pull a tiny comma liner stroke (see page 64) down from the bottom of each triangle.

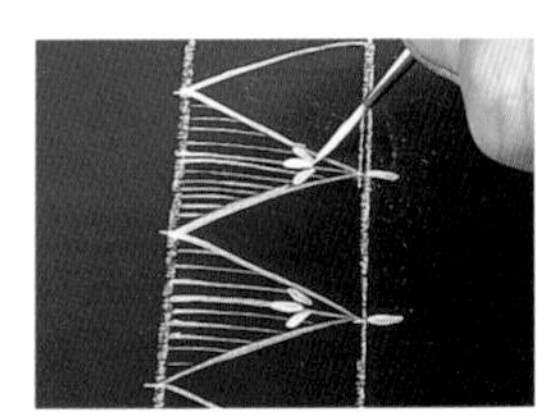

10 Use the same stroke to add a fleur-de-lis inside the point of each triangle.

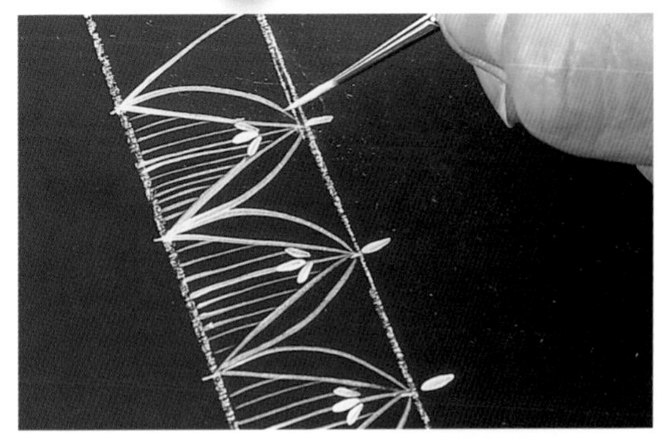

11 Paint a curved even line on either side of each triangle.

12 Paint tiny straight lines to crosshatch these new areas.

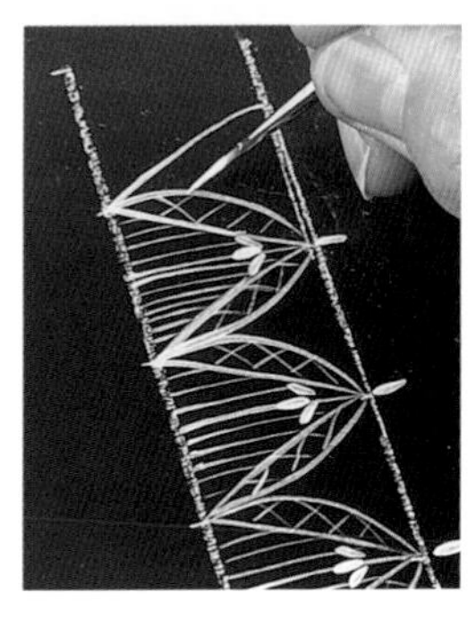

13 Dip a stylus in the white paint and add a dot below each fleur-de-lis.

Looking forward

When painting straight lines or dashes, work toward you as normal but look a little ahead of the brush to help cut out any wobbles.

These pretty primroses sit on a sponged background, and are detailed with linerwork.

of the brush acts as a reservoir for the paint. A medium-length liner is ideal for beginners, so start with a No. 0 or 1. A short liner is usually best for detail work.

For linerwork, use water to thin your paint so that it has an ink-like consistency. The round brushstrokes featured on pages 50–53 can also be used with a liner.

Pressured lines and commas

YOU WILL NEED

- **Palette: Admiral Blue**
- **Brushes: No. 1 liner**
- **Basic brush loading kit (page 49)**

1 Repeat steps 1–3 of Fine lines (page 62) to load your liner brush.

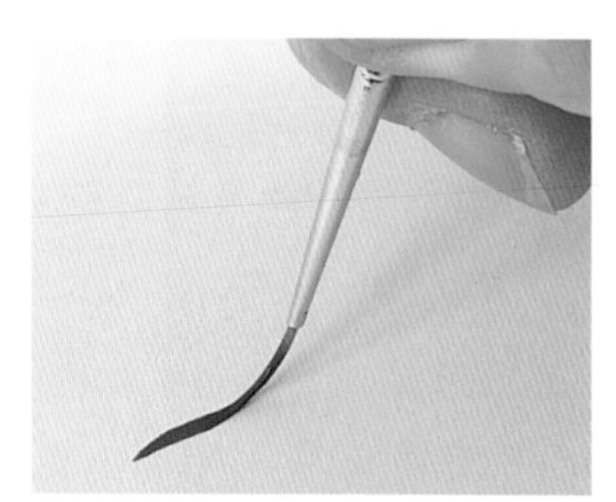

2 Hold the brush vertically over the surface to be painted and gradually lower it until the tip just touches the surface.

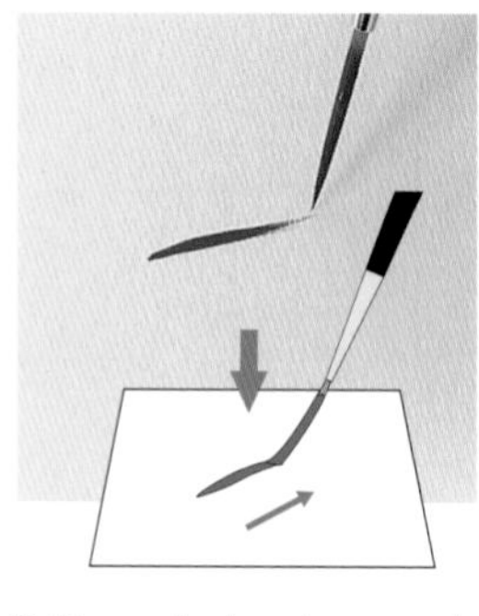

3 Draw the brush toward you, gradually applying more pressure to broaden the line.

4 Gradually release pressure toward the end of the stroke until just the tip of the brush touches the surface. Lift off.

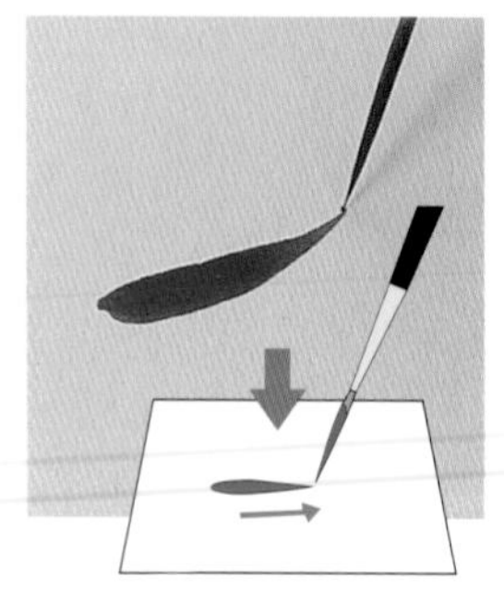

5 Practice applying varying amounts of pressure to the liner to achieve different results.

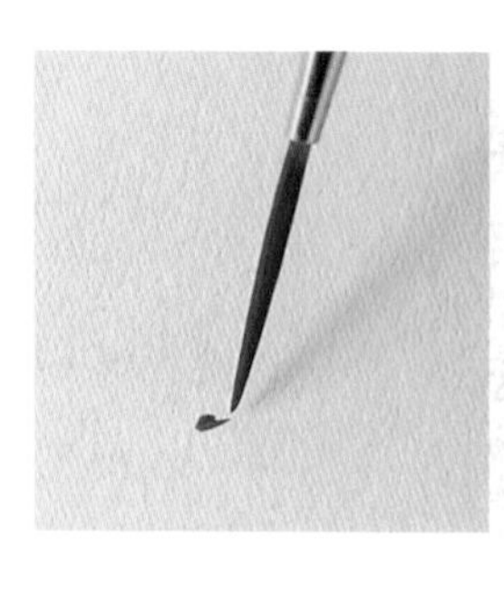

6 To make a tiny dot, simply touch the surface with the tip of the brush and release.

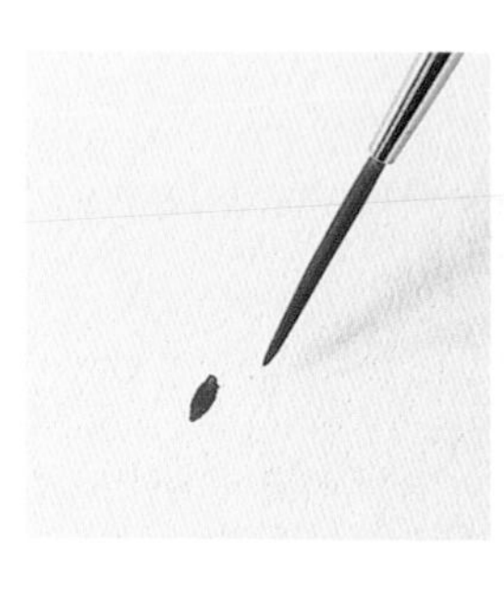

7 To make a larger dot, touch the surface with the tip of the brush and apply a little pressure before lifting off.

Liner-stroke thistle

YOU WILL NEED

- **Palette: Titanium White base with Admiral Blue, Shale Green, and Country Blue**
- **Brushes: No. 3 round brush, No. 1 liner**
- **Basic brush loading kit (page 49)**

1 Load a round brush with Admiral Blue, and paint in the flower head.

KEY → *Direction of brush*  *Heavy pressure*  *Medium pressure* ↓ *Light pressure*

The solid border, matching the color of the thistle motif, adds a nice finishing touch to this box, which could be used to store almost anything—from playing cards to cherished letters or recipes.

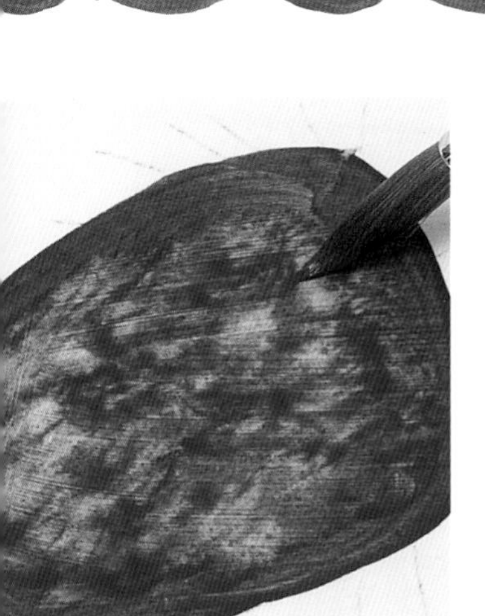

4 Blend on a dry palette to distribute the paint evenly through the brush. The paint should not travel more than two-thirds of the way up the bristles.

5 Roll the brush as you pull it through the paint on your dry palette so that the brush retains its shape. You should be able to see the paint on the brush, but it should not be overloaded.

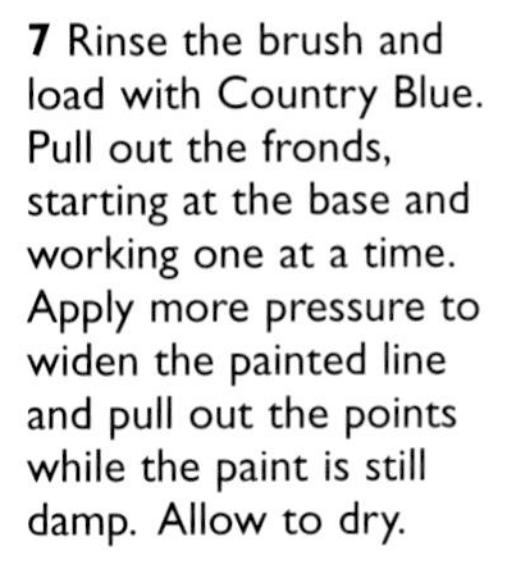

7 Rinse the brush and load with Country Blue. Pull out the fronds, starting at the base and working one at a time. Apply more pressure to widen the painted line and pull out the points while the paint is still damp. Allow to dry.

2 Rinse the brush and, before the blue is dry, pat it all over with the clean brush to give a textured effect. Wipe the brush on a clean paper towel if it picks up too much paint.

3 Thin some Shale Green paint with water to an inky consistency on the wet palette, and transfer some to the dry palette. Load a moistened liner by pulling it through the edge of the puddle of paint.

6 Pull the liner brush toward you in a long curve to form the stem. Apply more pressure to the brush to broaden the stem toward the middle. Paint the leaves, starting with the central line and pulling the side leaves out before the paint dries.

8 Rinse the brush and load with Hauser Dark Green. Using the tip of the liner only, pull a fine line along the center of each leaf. Repeat with Admiral Blue along the center of the lower petals.

Side loading

This technique, also known as floating color, involves the loading of paint and water onto a brush to achieve a smooth gradation of color, from the darkest on the front edge of the brush fading to nothing (water only) on the back of the brush. It takes some practice to get the loading just right.

Round-brush side load

YOU WILL NEED

- **Palette: Hauser Dark Green**
- **Generous Easi Float retarder mix (4–6 drops to 2 tsp/10ml water)**
- **Brushes: round brush**
- **Wet palette**

1 Moisten a round brush with the retarder mix. Press the brush down onto the wet palette, and flatten it to spread the bristles. The wet palette will maintain the right level of moisture in the brush.

2 Pull the edge of the brush through a puddle of paint on the wet palette. The paint should not go more than a quarter of the way across the brush at this stage. Press down on the wet palette and pull the brush toward you no more than 1 inch (2.5cm).

3 Repeat this several times on the same area, moving very slightly left and right to even out the paint on the bristles. The paint should not travel more than half-way across the brush and there should be no bubble of paint on the edge.

4 Hold the brush at about a 30°–40° angle from the surface and apply a stroke to release the paint from one edge of the brush only. Reload the brush with every stroke, but rinse if the paint travels too far across the brush.

Round-brush side load sunflower

YOU WILL NEED

- **Palette: Hauser Dark Green base with Terra Cotta, Antique Gold, Golden Straw, Taffy Cream, Burnt Umber, and Hauser Medium Green**
- **Brushes: No. 5 round brush, No. 1 liner**
- **Motif, tracing paper, masking tape, transfer paper, and stylus or empty ballpoint pen (optional)**
- **Generous Easi Float retarder mix (4–6 drops retarder to 2 tsp/10ml water)**

1 Either paint freehand or transfer a design to the prepared and base-coated surface (see page 25).

2 Load a round brush with Terra Cotta and paint straight commas (see page 50) to form the petals, starting from the center and pulling out. Leave to dry.

3 Rinse the brush and reload with Antique Gold. Add more comma petals, straight and curved, overlapping the dry petals in places. Do not fill the flower completely. Leave to dry.

***LEFT** A picture of symmetry, using double-loaded round brushstrokes and linerwork.*

***RIGHT** A bright sunflower plaque—just the place to hang your keys.*

4 Rinse the brush and load with Golden Straw. Fill in the gaps with more comma petals, overlapping the dry petals. Let dry.

5 Rinse the brush and side load with Taffy Cream. Add highlights to the edges of the Golden Straw petals and to the tips of other petals that would catch the light.

6 Rinse the brush and paint the center with Burnt Umber.

7 Before the center dries, use the tip of the brush to pat in Golden Straw for the pollen. Leave to dry.

8 Rinse the brush and side load with Terra Cotta. Use this to shade around the center.

9 Use a liner and Hauser Medium Green to paint in the stem line.

Side loading has been used on this decorative planter to add subtle detail to the petals of the daffodils.

Side loading a round brush may sound contradictory, but it is a very useful technique for shading and tinting small shapes.

When using a flat brush, keep in mind that you can use a wide brush for a narrow side load by adjusting the amount of paint you pick up, but you can't carry out a wide float with a narrow brush, so choose a brush appropriate to the width of float you need.

When applying the paint, use the whole width of the brush, holding your brush at a 30°–40° angle from the surface.

Flat-brush side load

YOU WILL NEED

- **Palette: Antique Teal**
- **Brushes: flat brush**
- **Generous Easi Float retarder mix (4–6 drops retarder to 2 tsp/10ml water)**
- **Wet palette**

1 Moisten a flat brush with the retarder mix and dip one corner of the brush into a puddle of Antique Teal on the wet palette. The paint should not go more than a quarter of the way across the brush at this stage.

2 Press down on the wet palette and pull the brush toward you no more than 1 inch (2.5cm). If the brush feels scratchy or drags, it needs more moisture.

3 Pull the brush toward you several times on the same area, moving very slightly left and right to even out the paint on the bristles. The paint should not travel more than halfway across the brush. If there is a bubble of paint on the leading edge of your brush keep blending until it disappears.

4 Turn the brush over and repeat on the other side of the paint-filled edge.

5 Holding the brush at about a 30°–40° angle, position your brush with the paint-filled edge where you want the deepest shading, and paint a stroke. One edge should be dark, and the other side fade to nothing. While the paint is wet you can repeat the covering to deepen the shading.

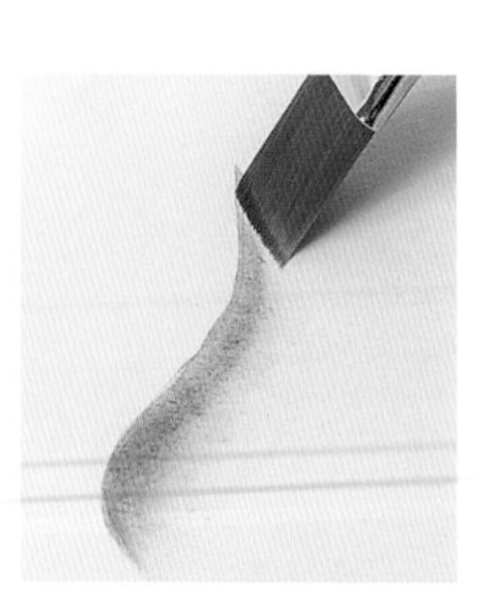

6 To widen the shaded area, repeat the stroke while it is still damp, starting a fraction away from the sharp edge.

7 For soft edges, start with the chisel edge of the brush touching the surface, with the clean edge away from the area to be shaded.

8 Turn the brush as you shade. Keep the paint on the edge to be shaded, and end on the chisel edge with the clean edge still to the outside.

***RIGHT** An inexpensive fabric notebook has been made special by the addition of a single flower.*

***ABOVE** This whole design uses just one color and is made up almost entirely of fine linerwork and side-load strokes.*

Flat-brush side load clematis

YOU WILL NEED

- **Palette: Raspberry base with Titanium White, Blue Mist, Black Plum, and Antique Teal**
- **Brushes: No. 8 or 10 flat brush, No. 1 liner**
- **Motif, tracing paper, masking tape, transfer paper, and stylus (optional)**
- **Generous Easi Float retarder mix (4–6 drops retarder to 2 tsp/10ml water)**
- **Wet palette**
- **Dry palette**

1 Either paint freehand or transfer a design to the prepared and base-coated surface (see page 25).

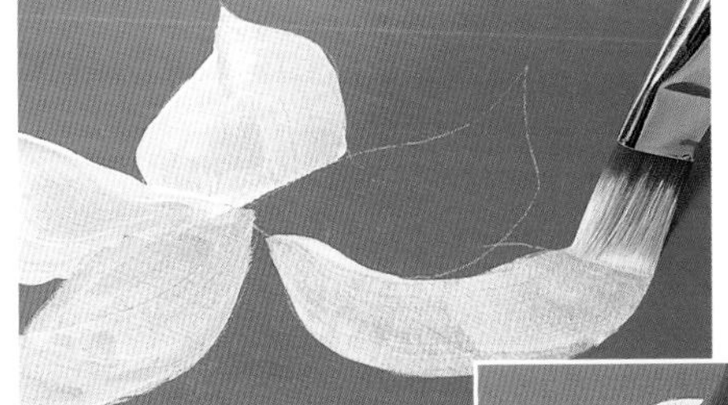

2 Load a flat brush with Titanium White and stroke in the petals. Leave to dry.

3 Rinse the brush and side load with Blue Mist. Apply strokes to separate the petals and paint under the fold.

4 Rinse and side load with Titanium White. Brush along the tops of the petals and the top edge of the fold. Leave to dry.

5 Load a liner with Black Plum and apply liner commas (see page 64) in the center of the flower.

6 Rinse the liner and load with Antique Teal. Paint an fine line (see page 62) for the stem.

7 Load the flat brush with Antique Teal as normal and paint wide ruffled stokes (see page 58) for each leaf.

The back edge will fade out as there is no paint on the side, so the result will be seamless. If the paint on the surface starts to dry, leave it to dry completely, then float more color on. Retarders are used to keep your paint open (damp), giving you more time to adjust your side load. Add two or three more drops of retarder to the retarder mix, or moisten the brush with a blending medium.

Back-to-back float

YOU WILL NEED

- **Palette: Country Red**
- **Brushes: flat brush**
- **Basic brush loading kit (page 49)**

1 Moisten a flat brush with retarder mix or water.

2 Dip one corner of the brush into a puddle of paint on the wet palette. The paint should not go more than a quarter of the way across the brush at this stage.

3 Press down on the wet palette and pull the brush toward you no more than 1 inch (2.5cm). The wet palette will maintain the right level of moisture in the brush. If the brush feels scratchy or drags, it needs more moisture.

4 Pull the brush toward you several times on the same area, moving slightly left and right to even out the paint on the bristles. The paint should not travel more than halfway across the brush. If a bubble of paint forms on the leading edge of your brush, keep blending until it disappears.

5 Turn the brush over and repeat on the other side of the paint-filled edge.

6 Moisten the area to be shaded with a clean, damp brush. Hold the brush at a 30°–40° angle with the paint-filled edge in the center, and apply a stroke.

7 While the paint is still damp, flip the brush over and repeat on the other side so that the two floats meet in the middle.

LEFT *Back-to-back floats are used to add shine to the waxy leaves of the oak tree that adorn this flower press.*

RIGHT *A simple peg shelf with a glazed bow and a flat-brush checkered border (see page 112).*

Glazed back-to-back float bow

Glazing is a means of adding subtle tints and accents to a painted design. The glaze is simply paint thinned with water.

YOU WILL NEED

- **Palette: Titanium White base with Light French Blue, French Grey-Blue, Deep Midnight Blue, Deep Burgundy, and Titanium White**
- **Brushes: No. 8 flat brush, No. 10 flat brush, No. 1 liner**
- **Basic brush loading kit (page 49)**
- **Motif, tracing paper, masking tape, transfer paper, and stylus (optional)**

1 Either paint freehand or transfer a design to the prepared and base-coated surface (see page 25).

2 Load a No. 8 flat brush with Light French Blue and paint in the bow. Leave to dry.

3 Rinse the brush and side load with French Grey-Blue (see page 68). Float the color under the upper areas to shade them. Leave to dry.

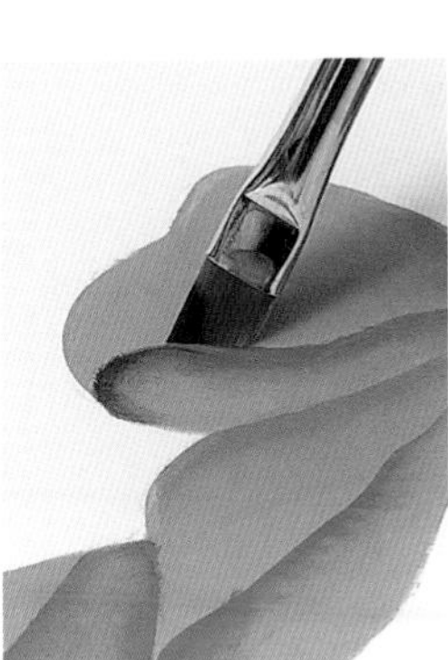

4 Rinse and side load with Deep Midnight Blue. Tuck the paint into the very darkest areas, over the previous shading.

5 Load a No. 10 flat brush with very thin Deep Burgundy and glaze in random tints.

6 Rinse the brush and side load with Titanium White. Float a highlight on the upper areas of the bow and knot. Apply a back-to-back float at the highest point of the bow.

Dip loading

Dip loading involves loading a brush with one color, and then dipping the tip into another color to release two colors in the one stroke. The two colors can be loaded on top of each other or on opposite corners of a flat brush, and when applied produce a streaked effect. The technique can be used for making a quick leaf or flower without the need for further shading.

Round-brush dip load

YOU WILL NEED

- **Palette: Country Red and Titanium White**
- **Brushes: round brush**
- **Basic brush loading kit (page 49)**

1 Load a round brush with the Country Red and dip the very tip of the loaded brush into the Titanium White.

2 Paint a stroke and see both colors come through.

Dip-loaded fan stroke

YOU WILL NEED

- **Palette: Country Red and Titanium White**
- **Brushes: round brush**
- **Basic brush loading kit (page 49)**

1 Load a round brush right up to the ferrule with the Country Red.

2 Dip the very tip of the loaded brush into the Titanium White.

3 Touch the tip of the brush on the surface to be painted and, keeping the brush upright, gradually press down until the hairs are flat on the surface with the handle at right angles.

4 Move the handle to the left and right spreading the bristles.

5 Push the brush forward about the length of the bristles.

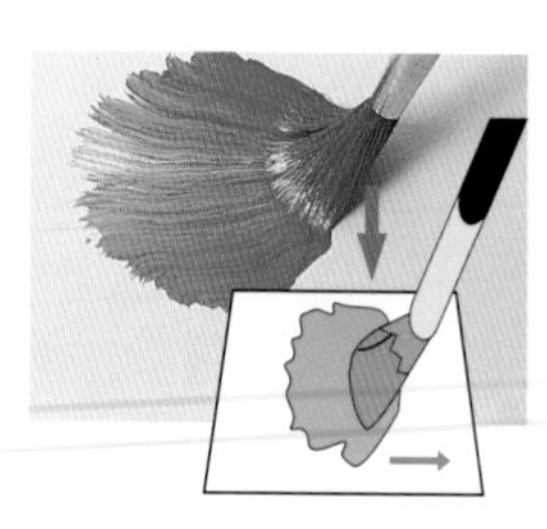

6 Pull the brush back to the start position and gradually lift the handle until the tip leaves the surface.

Flat-brush dip load

YOU WILL NEED

- **Palette: Raw Umber, Golden Straw, and Titanium White**
- **Brushes: flat brush**
- **Basic brush loading kit (page 49)**

1 Load the brush with Golden Straw, making sure there is no excess paint on the edges.

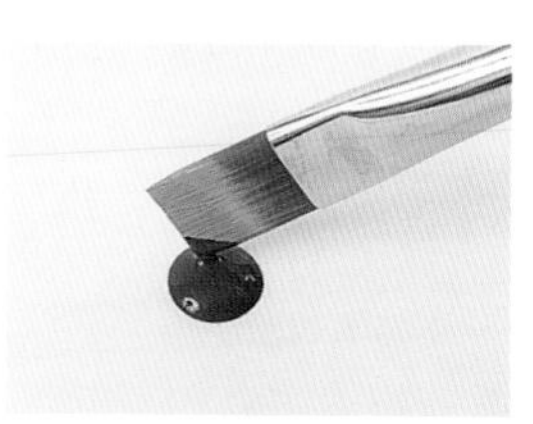

2 Dip one corner into the Raw Umber.

3 Turn the brush over and dip the other corner into the Titanium White.

KEY → *Direction of brush*  *Heavy pressure* *Medium pressure* *Light pressure*

LEFT *The round-brush comma leaves on this box are dip loaded with white on green.*

The fan stroke, when used with dip loading, is a spectacular, if unpredictable, stroke, and is great for painting variegated petals. However, this stroke is not good for your brush, so clean it thoroughly after use and take extra care to reshape the bristles.

RIGHT *A whitewashed dressing-table mirror.*

4 Dab the chisel edge lightly on the surface and pull it through a short line to lightly blend the two colors.

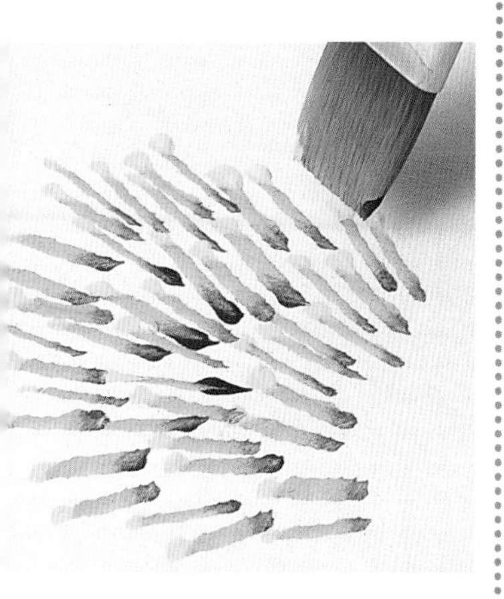

5 Build up a dome shape. This would make an ideal detail for a flower center.

Dip-loaded satin flower

YOU WILL NEED

- **Palette: Buttermilk base with Deep Burgundy, Titanium White, Antique Teal, and Green Mist**
- **Brushes: No. 3 or 5 round brush**
- **Basic brush loading kit (page 49)**
- **Pencil**

1 Draw two pencil lines at right angles to each other and add a third between the two.

2 Dip load a moistened round brush in Deep Burgundy followed by Titanium White.

3 Line up the brush with the central pencil line and apply a fan stroke. Reload and repeat on the other side of the line. Leave to dry.

4 Dip load the brush again and apply a fan stroke down the center of the painted flower.

5 Rinse the brush and dip load with Antique Teal followed by Green Mist.

6 Paint a curved comma (see page 50) at the base of the flower.

7 Add several comma leaves, reloading for each stroke.

also see the following pages
Applying the base coat 28–29 •**Transferring a design** 25 • **Brush loading and brushwork basics** 48–49 • **Dip loading** 72–73 • **Round brushstrokes** 50–53 • **Side loading** 66–71 **Shading and highlighting** 100–109 • **Liner brushstrokes** 62–65 • **The final touch** 114–117

Project 2

Daisy and strawberry planter

This striking planter uses techniques shown in Bases and basics and Essential strokes, as well as some simple blending and side loading. The dark background is a good foil for the stark white of the comma-stroke daisies and the bright red strawberries. The simple faux finish around the rim is an effective way to finish off.

YOU WILL NEED

- **Palette: Hauser Dark Green or Pine Green (Patio Paint) base with Hauser Medium Green, Hauser Light Green, Light Buttermilk, Golden Straw, Country Red, Black Plum, Raw Umber, Hauser Dark Green, Titanium White, and Terra Cotta**
- **Brushes: wide flat brush, No. 3 or 5 round brush, No. 6 or 8 flat brush or ¼-inch (0.5cm) angle brush, No. 1 liner, synthetic brush for varnishing**
- **Terra-cotta planter**
- **Multipurpose sealer (see Note)**
- **Fine-grade sandpaper**
- **Pansy motif**
- **Tracing paper**
- **Masking tape**
- **Transfer paper**
- **Stylus or empty ballpoint pen**
- **Basic brush loading kit (see page 49)**
- **Brush 'n' Blend blending medium**
- **Cotton swabs**
- **Matte varnish**

Note
Patio Paints are specifically designed for porous surfaces like terra-cotta. If you are using Pine Green Patio Paint for your base coat, you do not need to seal the surface first. If you are using Americana's Hauser Dark Green, seal the terra-cotta pot with a multipurpose sealer.

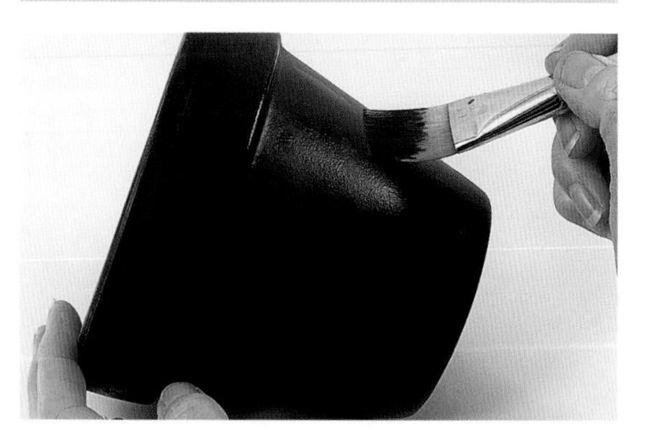

1 Use a wide flat brush to apply the base coat to the terra-cotta pot. Dry, sand, and repeat. Leave to dry.

2 Lightly transfer the daisy and strawberry motif to the pot. Don't transfer any of the thin lines, as it is easier to paint these in freehand than it is to follow drawn lines.

3 Load a round brush in Hauser Medium Green then dip with Hauser Light Green and apply comma strokes to the leaves. Allow to dry.

4 Rinse the round brush and dry it thoroughly. Without moistening it, load a little Light Buttermilk and use to highlight the leaves.

5 Rinse the round brush and paint each strawberry with Golden Straw. Dry and repeat.

6 Rinse the brush and moisten with blending medium. Apply a layer over each strawberry.

7 Rinse and paint in each strawberry with Country Red.

8 While the paint is still wet, use a cotton swab to dab out the center of each berry so the Golden Straw shows through. Dry thoroughly.

9 Coat the berries with another layer of blending medium. Side load a flat brush with Black Plum and shade the edges of the berries. Leave to dry.

10 Use a liner to paint in Raw Umber strawberry seeds. Leave to dry.

11 Highlight the berries with a dry round brush and Light Buttermilk as before. Leave to dry.

12 Rinse the liner and add Light Buttermilk crosshatching to the highlighted areas.

13 Rinse the liner and use it to highlight some of the seeds with a dot of Golden Straw. Leave to dry.

14 Load the round brush with Hauser Dark Green, and dip the tip in Hauser Light Green. Add calyxes.

15 Use round brush curved commas and Titanium White to paint the daisy petals at the back.

16 Rinse the brush and fill in the flower center with Golden Straw. Leave to dry.

17 Side load the flat or angle brush with Terra Cotta and shade the bottom of the flower center.

18 Rinse the round brush and dry thoroughly. Dry brush the center with Titanium White. Let dry.

19 Rinse and moisten the brush. Complete the front petals with Titanium White.

20 Rinse the liner and add the extra details using Hauser Medium Green.

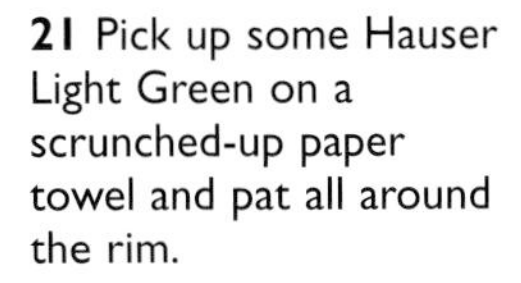

21 Pick up some Hauser Light Green on a scrunched-up paper towel and pat all around the rim.

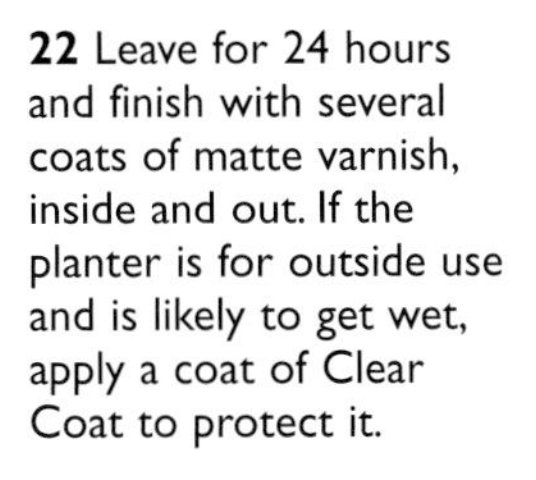

22 Leave for 24 hours and finish with several coats of matte varnish, inside and out. If the planter is for outside use and is likely to get wet, apply a coat of Clear Coat to protect it.

This decorative planter makes an attractive addition to the porch or patio.

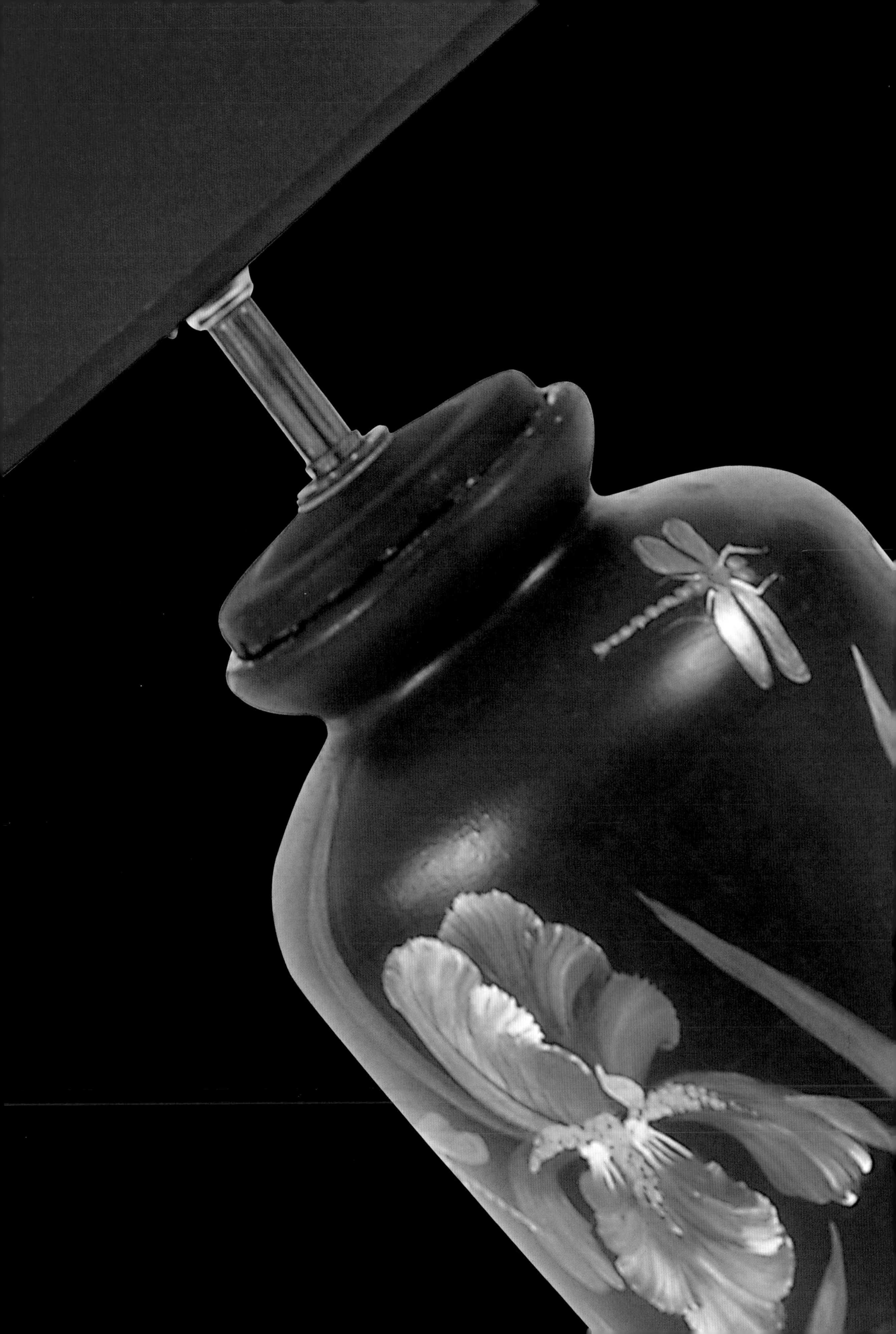

DEVELOPING STROKES

DEVELOPING STROKES

More advanced techniques, such as double and triple loading, allow you add shape and depth to your design, while an assortment of specialty brushes help create different kinds of textures.

This splendid stein has a Bavarian-style stroke design.

Round-brush double and triple loading

A number of folk art designs rely on using more than one color on the brush. Different from dip loading, double and triple loading actually blends the extra colors into the brush to achieve different and more subtle effects. A round brush can be double loaded in two ways. Adding a second color to a fully loaded brush gives a soft transition of color, whereas loading two colors separately allows

Double loading: technique 1

YOU WILL NEED

- **Palette: Antique Teal and Green Mist**
- **Brushes: round brush**
- **Basic brush loading kit (see page 49)**

1 Load a round brush with paint and blend as normal. Press the tip down on the dry palette to flatten the end slightly.

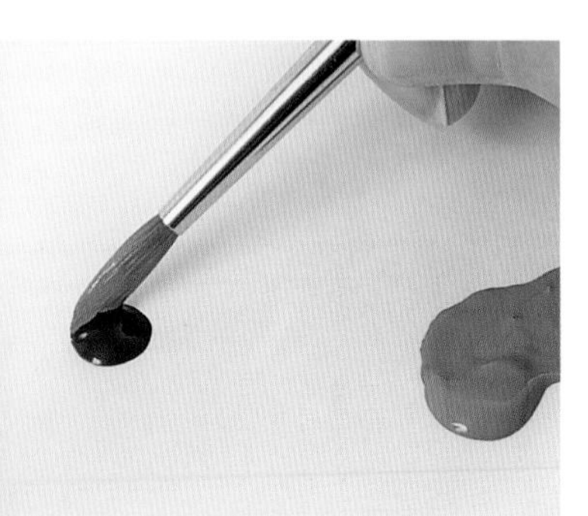

2 Holding the brush at a low angle, dip one side only into the second color.

3 Blend very lightly on the dry palette.

4 Hold the brush at a 30°–40° angle from the surface and apply a stroke to release both paint colors. Reload before each stroke.

Double loading: technique 2

YOU WILL NEED

- **Palette: Hauser Dark Green and Cadmium Yellow**
- **Brushes: round brush**
- **Basic brush loading kit (see page 49)**

1 Moisten a round brush as usual and press the tip down on the dry palette to flatten the end slightly.

2 Pull the slightly flattened brush through the edge of a puddle of paint on the wet palette.

3 Blend lightly on the dry palette to distribute the paint, which should not travel more than halfway across the brush.

4 Turn the brush over and pull the other edge through the second color and blend as before.

5 Hold the brush at a 30°–40° angle from the surface and apply a stroke to release both paint colors. Reload before each stroke.

This round-brush triple-loaded Chrysanthemum is a quick design to decorate a plain item—here, a key holder.

for more distinction between the two.

To triple load a round brush, the first color is fully loaded and the two subsequent colors loaded to each side of the brush.

Triple loading

YOU WILL NEED

- **Palette: Burnt Orange, True Ochre, and Moon Yellow**
- **Brushes: round brush**
- **Basic brush loading kit (see page 49)**

1 Load a round brush with paint and blend as normal. Press the tip down on the dry palette to flatten the end slightly.

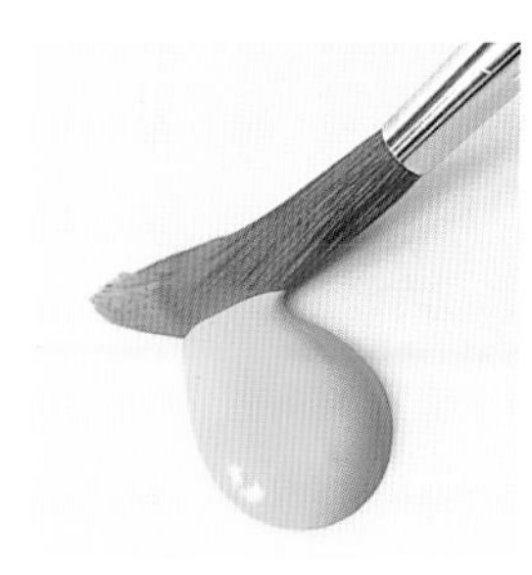

2 Holding the brush at a low angle, dip one side only into the second color.

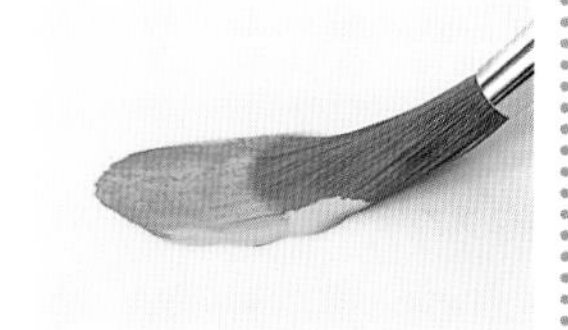

3 Blend lightly on a wet or dry palette to distribute the paint, which should not travel more than one third of the way across the brush.

4 Turn the brush over. Pull the other edge through the third color, and blend as before.

5 Hold the brush at a 30°–40° angle from the surface and apply a stroke to release all three paint colors. Reload before each stroke.

Round-brush triple-loaded chrysanthemum

YOU WILL NEED

- **Palette: Buttermilk base, with Burnt Orange, Pineapple, and Golden Straw**
- **Brushes: No. 3 or 5 round brush**
- **Basic brush loading kit (see page 49)**

1 Load a round brush with Burnt Orange and paint a large oval for the center of the flower.

2 Before the Burnt Orange dries, rinse the round brush and pat a little Pineapple onto the upper part of the center. Leave to dry.

3 Rinse the round brush. Triple load with Burnt Orange followed by Golden Straw on one side and Pineapple on the other.

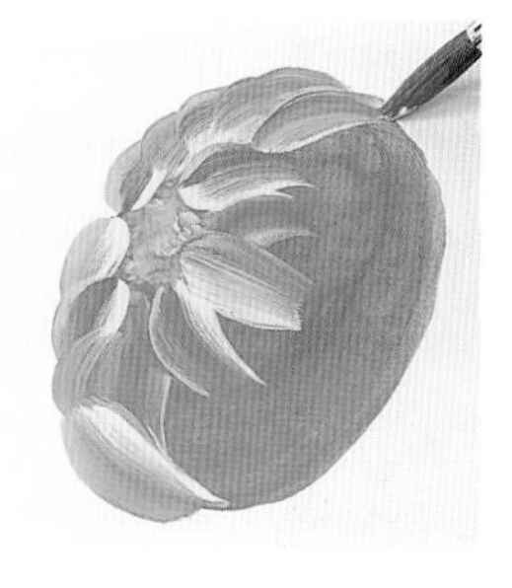

4 Starting at the back and working on alternate sides, pull curved comma strokes (see page 50) following the shape of the center. Work with the Golden Straw to the outside of the flower.

5 Add comma petals curling out from the base. When you reload, remember to add the lighter colors to the same sides. You may not need to reload the Burnt Orange every time, but always blend the brush before adding the lighter colors.

Flat-brush double and triple loading

Double and triple loading techniques are traditionally used with a round brush, but double or triple loading a flat brush gives interesting and attractive strokes and it is well worth practising both. In fact, I find it much easier to multi load a

Double loading: technique 1

YOU WILL NEED

- **Palette: Hauser Dark Green and Reindeer Moss Green**
- **Brushes: flat brush**
- **Basic brush loading kit (see page 49)**

1 Moisten a flat brush and pull the edge of the brush through the first color on the wet palette. The paint should not go more than one third of the way across the brush.

2 Turn the brush over and pick up the second color on the other side.

3 Press down on the wet palette and pull the brush toward you no more than 1 inch (2.5cm). Pull the brush toward you several times on the same area, moving a little left and right to even out the paint on the bristles.

4 Turn the brush over, and repeat, adding more paint if required. There should be a smooth transition from one color to the other.

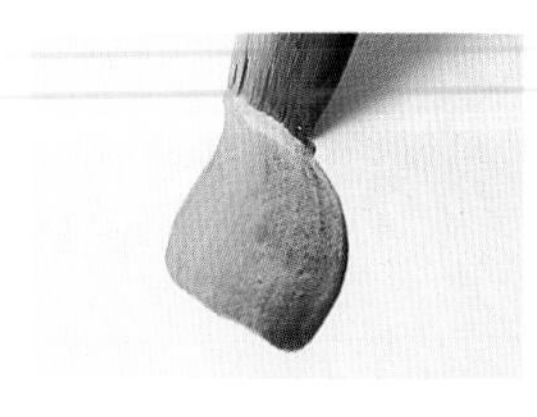

5 Hold the brush almost upright and paint a stroke.

Double loading: technique 2

YOU WILL NEED

- **Palette: Hauser Dark Green and Reindeer Moss Green**
- **Brushes: flat brush**
- **Basic brush loading kit (see page 49)**

1 Load a flat brush with paint and blend as usual.

2 Pick up a second color on one corner of the brush only.

3 Press down on the wet palette and pull the brush toward you no more than 1 inch (2.5cm). Pull the brush toward you several times on the same area, moving very slightly left and right to even out the paint on the bristles.

4 Move to a fresh place on the palette, turn the brush over, and blend again. Add more paint if required. There should be a smooth transition across the brush from one color to the other.

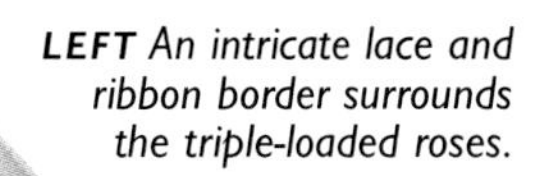

***LEFT** An intricate lace and ribbon border surrounds the triple-loaded roses.*

***RIGHT** Double-loaded flat-brush roses finish this pretty pot pourri basket.*

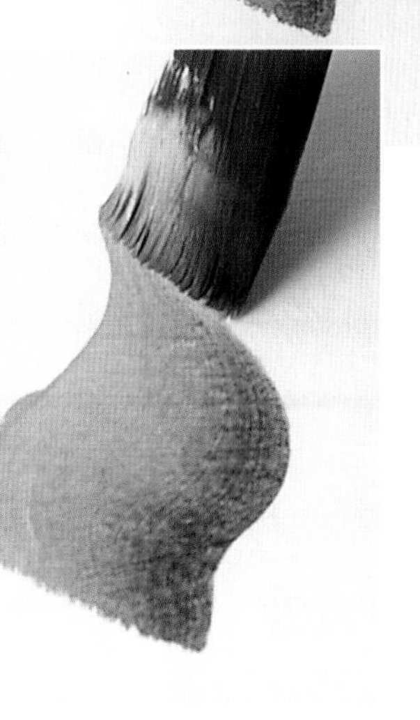

5 Hold the brush almost upright and paint a stroke to release the two blended colors.

Triple loading: technique 1

YOU WILL NEED

- **Palette: Antique Teal, Green Mist, and Pineapple**
- **Brushes: flat brush**
- **Basic brush loading kit (see page 49)**

1 Load a flat brush with paint and blend as normal.

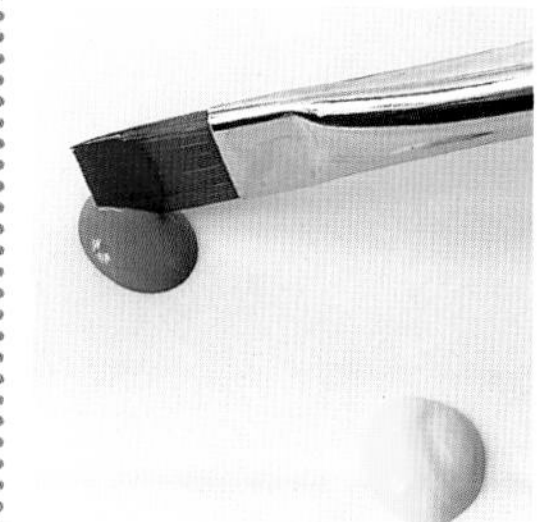

2 Pick up the second color on one side of the brush only.

3 Press down on the wet palette and pull the brush toward you no more than 1 inch (2.5cm). Pull the brush toward you several times on the same area, moving very slightly left and right to even out the paint on the bristles.

4 Turn the brush over and pick up the third color on the other side.

5 Blend again. There should be a smooth transition across the brush from one color to the other.

6 Hold the brush almost upright and paint a stroke to release all three blended colors.

flat brush than a round one. To achieve the best results with flat-brush multi loading, keep blending the paint into the brush until it is really full, almost up to the ferrule. Remember that the transition between the colors should be gradual but distinct.

Triple loading: technique 2

YOU WILL NEED

- **Palette: Antique Teal, Green Mist, and Pineapple**
- **Brushes: flat brush**
- **Basic brush loading kit (see page 49)**

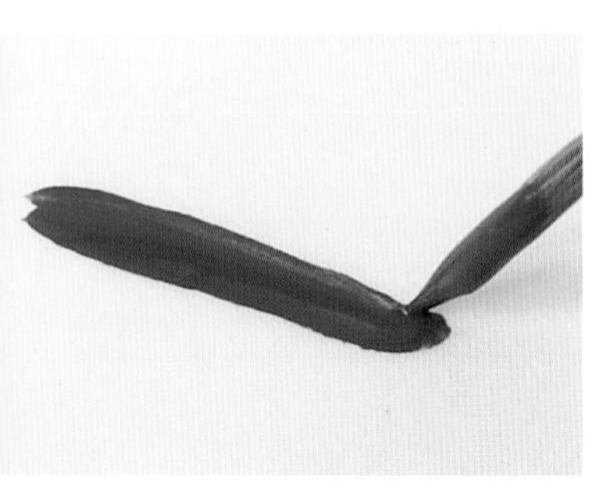

1 Using a stylus, the end of a paint brush or a round brush, transfer a line of Antique Teal to a wet palette.

2 Moisten a flat brush, and pick up some Green Mist on one side of the brush only and blend lightly.

3 Turn the brush over and pick up the third color, Pineapplem on the other side. Blend lightly.

4 Position the the middle of the brush, which has no paint on it yet, at the start of your line of Antique Teal, and pull the brush along to pick up the paint.

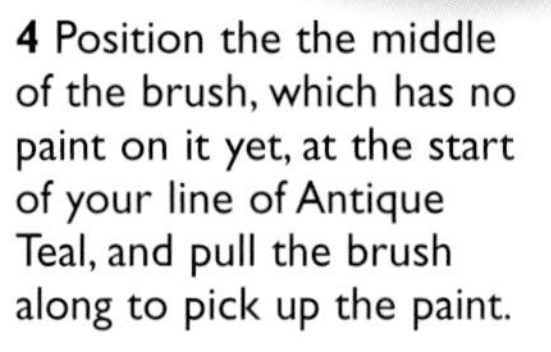

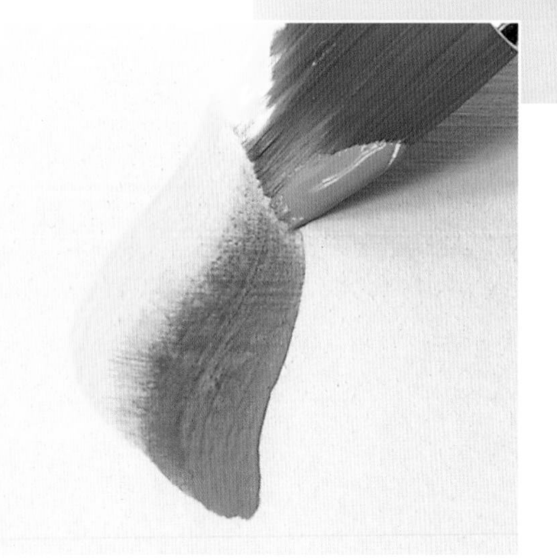

5 Press down on the wet palette and pull the brush toward you no more than 1 inch (2.5cm). Pull the brush toward you several times on the same area, moving very slightly left and right to even out the paint on the bristles.

There should be a smooth transition across the brush from one color to the other.

6 Hold the brush almost upright and paint a stroke to release all three blended colors.

LEFT *Double-loaded rosebuds and leaves encircle this pretty plate.*

RIGHT *A spray of similar rosebuds and leaves are painted on a decorative plant pot, demonstratng how a particular motif can be adapted to suit different objects and designs.*

Double- and triple-loaded rosebud and leaves

YOU WILL NEED

- **Palette: Buttermilk base, with Deep Burgundy, Titanium White, Antique Teal, and Green Mist**
- **Brushes: No. 8 flat brush, No. 1 liner**
- **Basic brush loading kit (see page 49)**

1 Double load a flat brush, using technique 1 or 2, with Deep Burgundy and Titanium White.

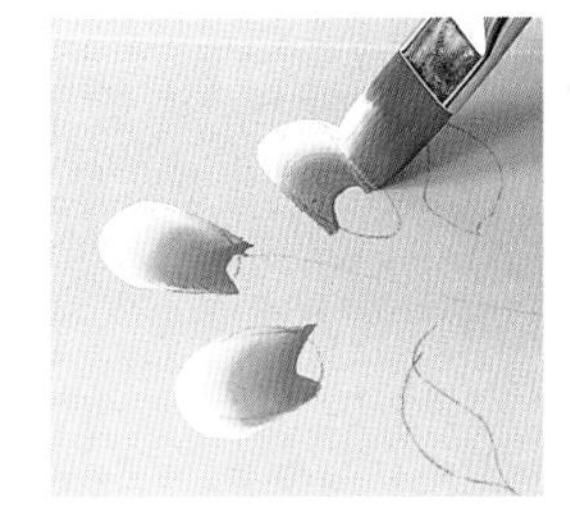

2 Place the brush on the chisel edge halfway up the left side of the oval flower, or the right side if you are left-handed. Paint a broad arc up and around following the shape of the oval, finishing on the opposite side on the chisel edge (see Crescent, page 58).

3 Reload the brush in the same way and, starting in the same place, follow the shape down and around under the first stroke, finishing where you ended the first stroke. Repeat for each rosebud.

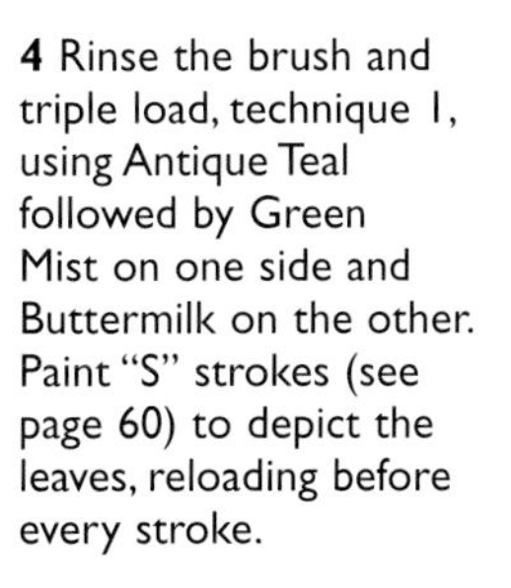

4 Rinse the brush and triple load, technique 1, using Antique Teal followed by Green Mist on one side and Buttermilk on the other. Paint "S" strokes (see page 60) to depict the leaves, reloading before every stroke.

5 Using Antique Teal and Green Mist, paint in the stalks with a liner.

Specialty brushes

As well as the basic set of brushes, consisting of rounds, flats, and liners, there are a number of specialty brushes designed for particular techniques. Each brush has a different use or gives a different effect. Some of these can be mixed and matched for shading and highlighting effects (see pages 100–107), while others make distinctive.

Stippler

A stippler, sometimes called a fabric scrubber, is usually used dry, that is not moistened and with a minimum of paint. The stippler is round with a domed head and fairly stiff bristles. It is often used for foliage techniques and some forms of highlighting. It can also be used for textures such as fur.

YOU WILL NEED

- **Palette: Golden Straw**
- **Brushes: stippler**
- **Wet palette**
- **Dry palette**
- **Paper towel**

1 Do not moisten the stippler. Load it with paint and work the paint into the brush on a dry palette.

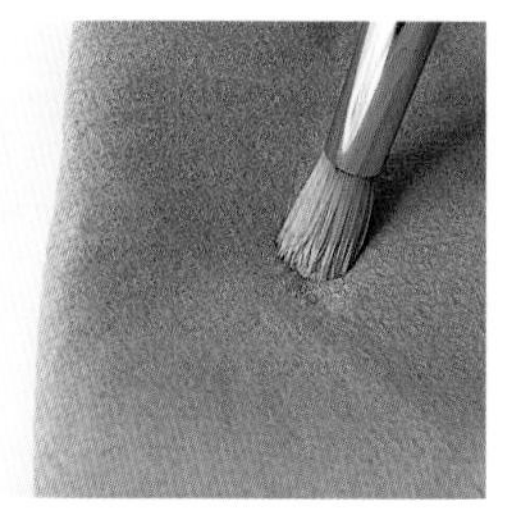

2 Work the brush into a paper towel to remove excess paint.

3 Hold the brush upright and dab, or pounce, it evenly over the surface.

4 Use a circular scrubbing motion to blend the applied paint.

Duckling

YOU WILL NEED

- **Palette: Shale Green base, with Raw Umber, Light Cinnamon, Light Buttermilk, Yellow Ochre, Antique Gold, Soft Black, and Blue-Grey Mist**
- **Brushes: No. 3 round brush, No. 2 round brush, No. 8 stippler, No. 1 liner**
- **Basic brush loading kit (see page 49)**
- **Motif, tracing paper, masking tape, transfer paper, and stylus**
- **Brush 'n' Blend blending medium**

1 Transfer a design to the prepared and base-coated surface (see page 25).

2 Use a No. 3 round brush to apply blending medium to the feet and legs of the duckling.

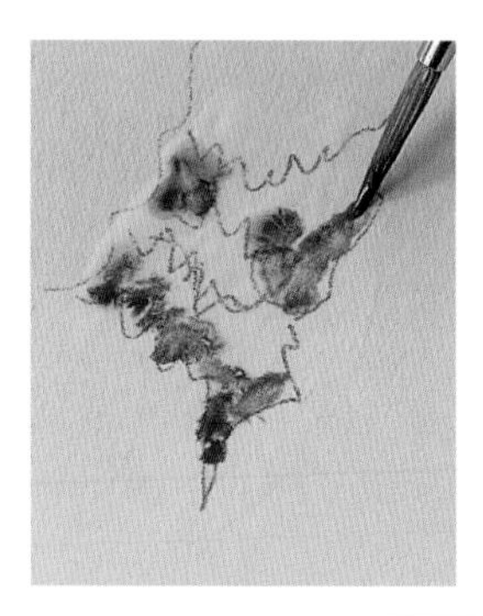

3 Load a No. 2 round brush with Raw Umber and dab in small areas over the feet and legs. Pick up some Light Cinnamon (there is no need to rinse the brush), and repeat.

LEFT *The different textures in this farmyard design were made using a variety of brush techniques, including stippling. The chicks "stepping out" of the frame adds another dimension.*

RIGHT *A trio of stippled ducklings with a spray of leaves.*

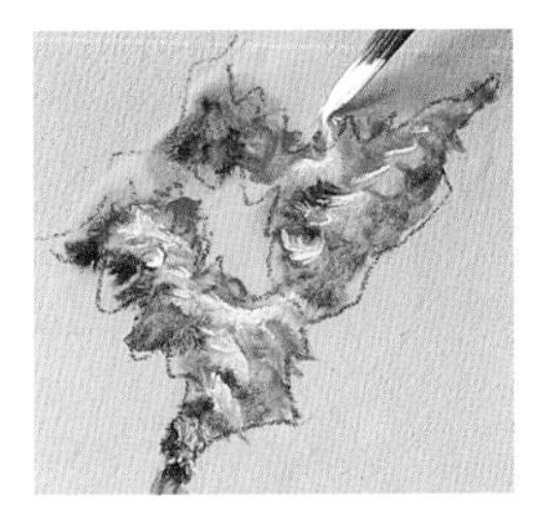

4 Rinse the brush and dab in small areas of Light Buttermilk. Gently blend all the feet and leg colors while the paint is still wet, so that the colors merge. Leave to dry.

5 Use a dry stippler loaded with Yellow Ochre to paint in the body of the duckling. Use a circular blending stroke to produce a fluffy texture. Some of the background color will show through. Leave to dry.

6 Clean as much of the Yellow Ochre off the stippler as possible on a paper towel. Load the dry stippler with Antique Gold and stipple all over the body shape, making the covering lighter toward the middle. Leave to dry.

7 Wipe the stippler as clean as possible and load with Light Buttermilk. Highlight the upper center of the body and head.

8 Rinse the No 2 round brush, load it with Soft Black, and paint the eye. Leave to dry.

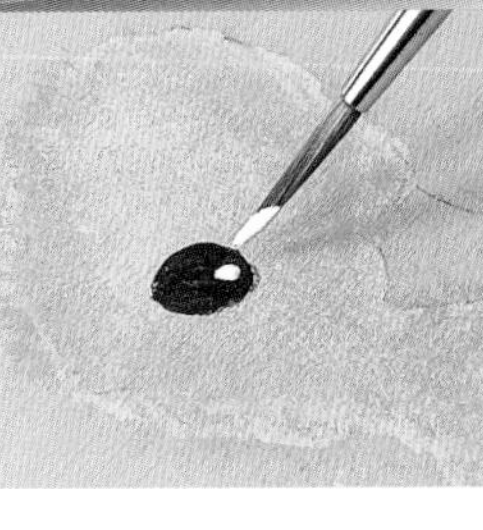

9 Rinse the brush and dot in a highlight of Light Buttermilk.

10 Rinse the brush and use it to paint the beak with Blue-Grey Mist and let dry.

11 Side load the No 3 round brush with Raw Umber (see page 66) and shade under the top part of the beak.

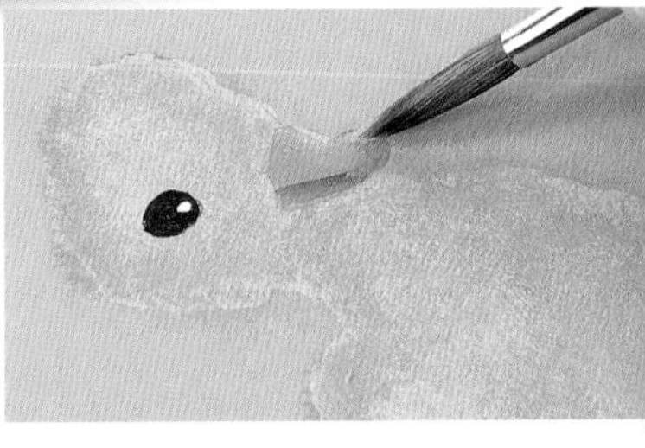

12 Rinse and side load with Light Buttermilk to highlight the top of the beak.

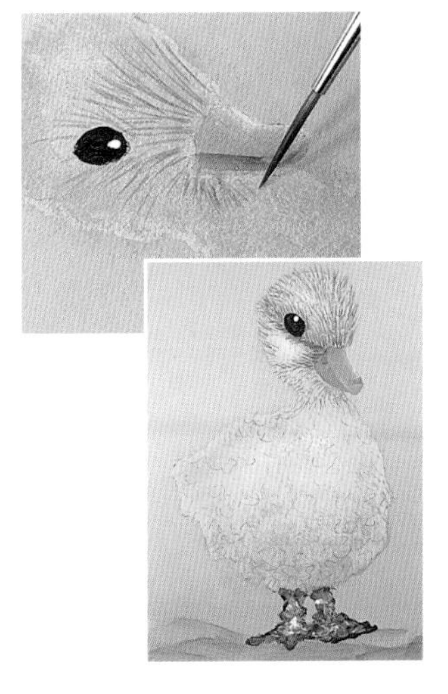

13 Load a liner with Raw Umber. Pull thin strokes away from the beak across the head and add some random squiggles to "fluff" up the body.

Topiary and birdhouses are a key feature of this peg shelf. Various strokes and techniques are employed, along with stippler and deerfoot brushes.

Deerfoot

A similar brush to the stippler (see page 86), the deerfoot has an angled top. The tip can be lightly loaded, dry, or the tip and heel can be loaded with different colors to create variegated foliage. It can also be used to tap in "fuzzy" leaves or blossom on a tree.

Single-color deerfoot stroke

YOU WILL NEED

- **Palette: Golden Straw**
- **Brushes: deerfoot**
- **Basic brush loading kit (see page 49)**
- **Paper towel**

1 Do not moisten the deerfoot. Load the dry brush with paint.

2 Work the paint into the brush on a dry palette.

3 Dab the brush over a paper towel to remove excess paint.

4 Hold the brush almost upright and dab, or pounce, it evenly over the surface.

Two-color deerfoot stroke

YOU WILL NEED

- **Palette: Golden Straw, Hauser Medium Green**
- **Brushes: deerfoot**
- **Basic brush loading kit (see page 49)**

1 Without moistening the deerfoot, load the first color onto the toe, the longest part of the brush.

2 Turn the brush over and load the heel, the shorter part, with the second color.

3 Tap the brush on a dry palette to blend the colors slightly.

4 Hold the brush almost upright and apply to the surface with a pouncing, dabbing, movement.

strokes in their own right. Here I provide an overview of the main uses for each brush, but you will undoubtedly find your particular favorites for specific effects. The filbert brush, for example, makes lovely petals and foliage effects. While experimenting with these, I

***RIGHT** A simple deerfoot stroke makes this topiary tree, decorating an octagonal coaster.*

Deerfoot topiary tree

YOU WILL NEED

- **Palette: Titanium White base, with Burnt Umber, Hauser Medium Green, Hauser Dark Green, Olive Green, and Terra Cotta**
- **Brushes: No. 1 liner, No. ¼-inch (0.5cm) deerfoot, No. 10 flat brush**
- **Basic brush loading kit (see page 49)**

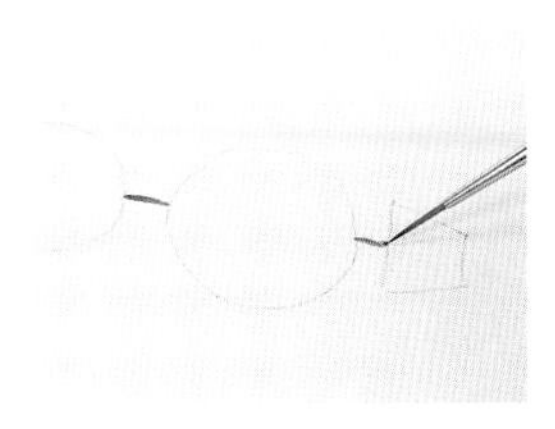

1 Paint in Burnt Umber tree trunks using a liner (see page 62).

2 Take a dry deerfoot and pick up Hauser Medium Green on the toe and Hauser Dark Green on the heel. Dab lightly on a dry palette to blend.

3 Working on the top circle with the lighter color at the top, dab the brush across the top arc. Work your way down the circle, keeping the shape until the whole circle is filled. Refill your brush and dab in the lower circle. Leave to dry.

4 Wipe the deerfoot on a paper towel. Do not rinse it. Dip the toe into Olive Green and blend on the dry palette. Work lightly into the upper part of the center of each circle. Leave to dry.

5 Load a flat brush with Terra Cotta as normal and paint in the pot, stroking from side to side. Leave to dry.

6 Side load the flat brush with Burnt Umber (see page 68) and shade each side of the pot.

discovered the filbert was also ideal for producing a fur effect, which I have used for the teddy on page 91. Once you have started building a set of specialty brushes, take the time to play around with them, and you may discover new techniques and paint effects of your own.

Filbert

This is really a flat brush with a round tip. It can be used for base painting petals or leaves, and is very flexible for getting into tight places. To cover a smaller area, use less of the brush by lifting it a little. The filbert can also be used as a round brush for painting comma petals or leaves. Use the round brush strokes (see pages 50–53), but keep them more compact.

YOU WILL NEED

- **Palette: Sapphire**
- **Brushes: filbert**
- **Basic brush loading kit (see page 49)**

1 Load a moistened filbert by pulling it through a puddle of paint. Turn the brush over and pull it through the paint again.

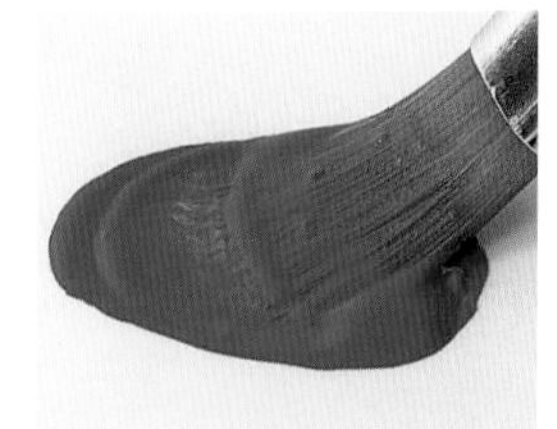

2 Blend on a dry palette to distribute the paint evenly through the brush.

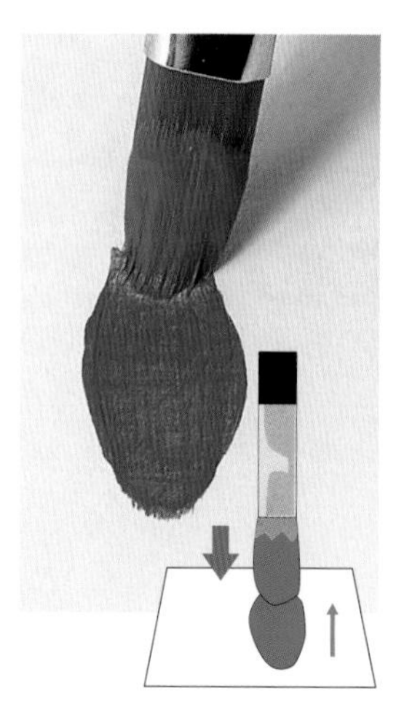

3 Place the tip of the brush on the surface to be painted and press down on the flat side. Pull the brush toward you, gradually turning and lifting to end on the edge of the brush. Lift off.

Filbert hydrangea

YOU WILL NEED

- **Palette: Payne's Grey base with Blue Violet, Sapphire, Titanium White, and Hauser Light Green**
- **Brushes: No. 10 flat brush, No. 8 filbert**
- **Basic brush loading kit (see page 49)**
- **Stylus**

1 Use a flat brush to paint random strokes in a round area, picking up, alternately, Blue Violet and Sapphire without rinsing the brush. Do not make the base too solid. Leave to dry.

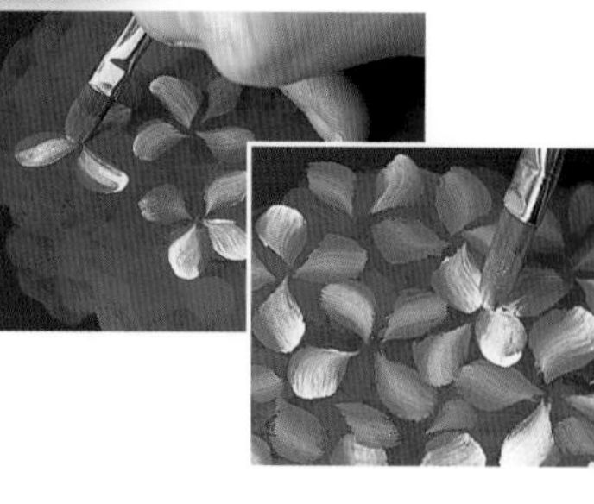

2 Load a moistened filbert with Sapphire, then dip the very tip lightly in Titanium White. Randomly paint groups of four curved commas (see page 50). Try not to make the pattern look too regimented.

3 Continue painting groups of petals to cover the whole base circle. Add the occasional individual petal to fill in gaps. Leave to dry.

4 Pick up Hauser Light Green on the end of a stylus and use it to dot the center of each group of petals.

KEY → *Direction of brush* ⬇ *Heavy pressure* ⬇ *Medium pressure* ↓ *Light pressure*

LEFT *The domed lid of this rounded ceramic bowl makes an ideal base for the round head of a hydrangea.*

RIGHT *The filbert fur technique can be applied to teddies of all shapes and sizes.*

Filbert fur teddy bear

YOU WILL NEED

- **Palette: Buttermilk base with Honey Brown, Asphaltum, Country Red, and Light Buttermilk**
- **Brushes: No. 8 filbert, No. 8 flat brush, No 1 liner, ¼-inch (0.5cm) deerfoot or stippler**
- **Basic brush loading kit (see page 49)**
- **Motif, tracing paper, masking tape, transfer paper, and stylus (optional)**

1 Either paint freehand or transfer a design to the prepared and base-coated surface (see page 25).

2 Moisten a filbert, but only lightly. For this technique the brush should be barely moist. Load with Honey Brown.

3 Blend the paint into the brush on a dry palette.

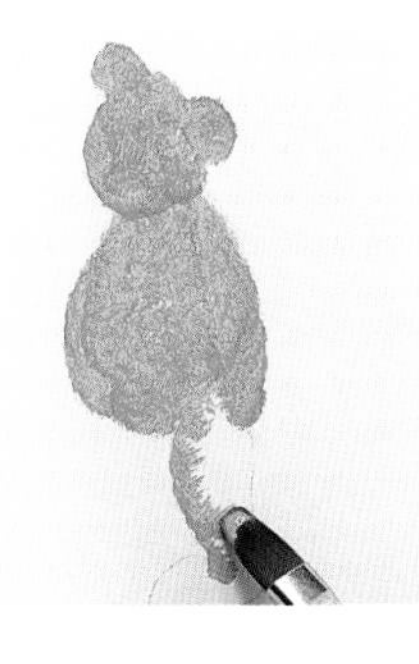

4 Apply the paint to the surface by dabbing, or pouncing, the brush. Work on one section at a time and do not go back over an area once it has started to dry. When complete, leave to dry.

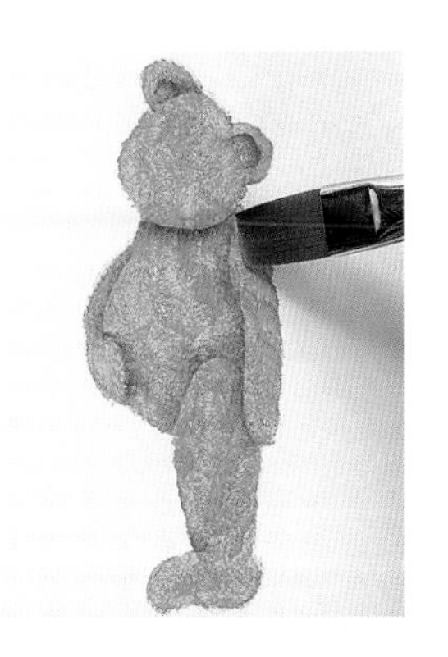

5 Side load a flat brush with Asphaltum (see page 68) and shade behind the front sections and along the lower edge of the bear.

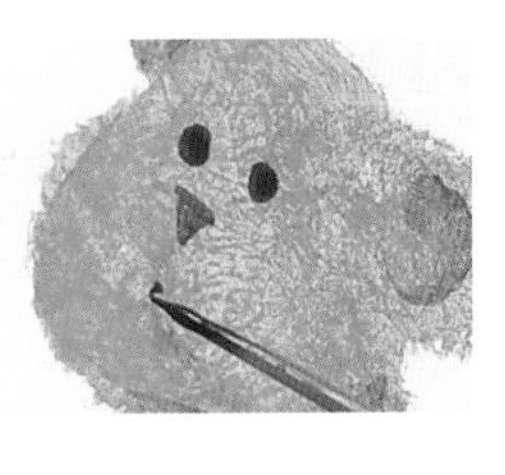

6 Load a liner with Asphaltum, and add the face details (see pages 62–65). Leave to dry.

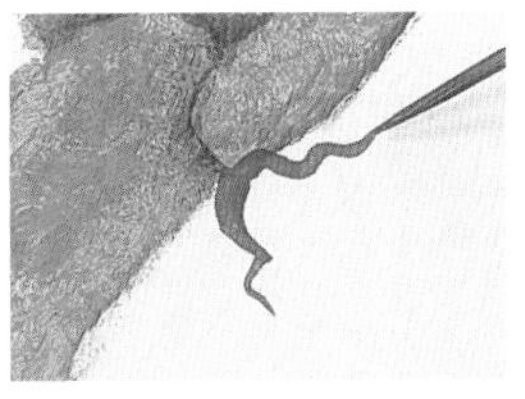

7 Rinse the liner and load with Country Red. Paint the tie in the bear's hand.

8 Rinse again and load with Light Buttermilk. Dot a highlight in each eye.

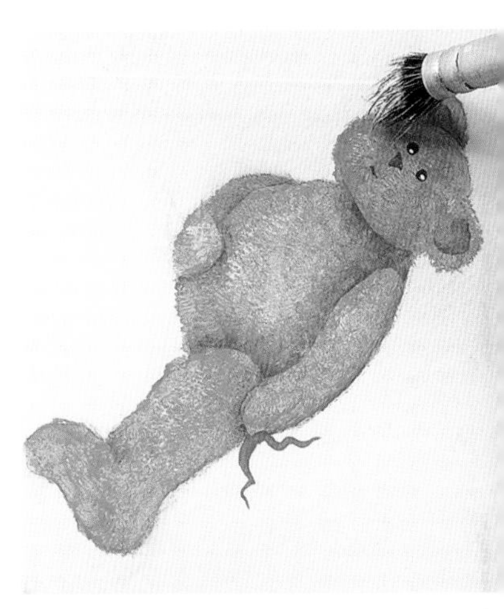

9 Load a deerfoot or stippler (see pages 86 and 88) with Light Buttermilk, and dry brush highlights all over the bear. Dry.

10 Rinse the flat brush, side load with a very thin Country Red and water mix, and add an arc to the bear's cheek.

Rake

A rake, or comb, is like a row of liners, and can be used as such to make short work of lined designs like grass, hair, or fur. It is basically a flat brush with a good body of hair at the base that has been thinned out at the top.

YOU WILL NEED

- **Palette: Hauser Medium Green and Asphaltum**
- **Brushes: rake**
- **Basic brush loading kit (see page 49)**

1 Thin some Hauser Medium Green with water to the consistency of ink, and make a puddle on the wet palette. Load a moistened rake with a little paint at a time by pulling it through the edge of a puddle. The brush should be filled, but not overloaded.

2 Touch the tips of the brush on a dry palette to test the load and ensure the paint is not too thick or too runny.

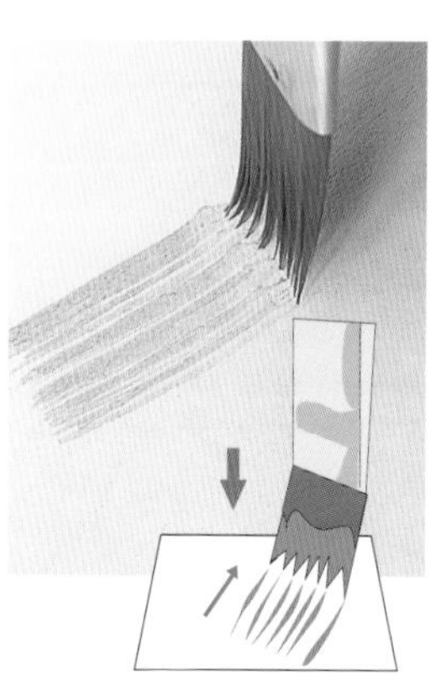

3 Hold the brush upright and gradually lower the tips onto the surface. When just touching, pull the brush toward you, keeping it upright.

4 Overlap a number of slightly outward curving strokes to paint a patch of grass.

5 Wiggle the brush as you pull each stroke to imitate hair, again overlapping the strokes.

Filbert rake

This brush is a combination of a filbert and a rake. The curved shape leaves a softer edge than the straight rake. Like the rake, it is generally used to create a row of lines for grass, fur, or hair.

YOU WILL NEED

- **Palette: Evergreen**
- **Brushes: filbert rake**
- **Basic brush loading kit (see page 49)**

1 Thin some Evergreen with water to the consistency of ink, making a puddle on the wet palette. Load a moistened filbert rake with a little paint at a time, by pulling it through the edge of a puddle. The brush should be filled but not overloaded.

KEY → *Direction of brush*  *Heavy pressure*  *Medium pressure* ↓ *Light pressure*

LEFT *This cute little bird on a Christmas ornament is "fluffed up" with layers of blending gel and tiny brushstrokes formed with a filbert rake.*

RIGHT *This stunning lamp base is decorated with fan-stroke irises. The shade is finished with delicate dragonflies.*

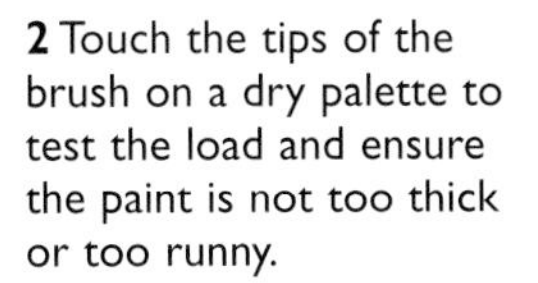

2 Touch the tips of the brush on a dry palette to test the load and ensure the paint is not too thick or too runny.

3 Hold the brush upright and gradually lower the tips onto the surface. When just touching, pull the brush toward you, keeping it upright.

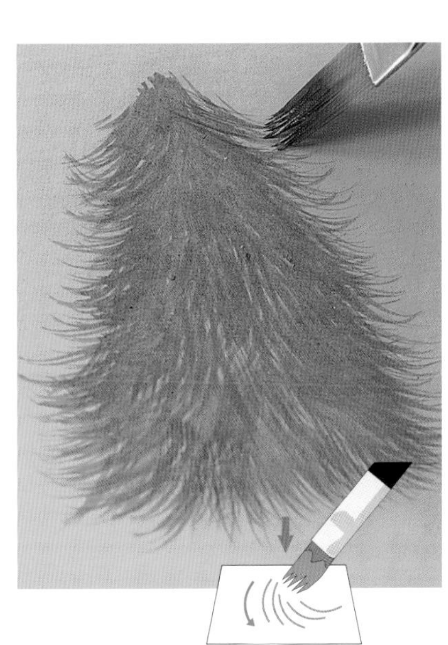

4 Overlap straight strokes in the center and outward curved strokes to paint a fir tree.

Mop

The mop is a soft, usually round-headed, brush used dry for blending wet areas.

YOU WILL NEED

- **Palette: Deep Burgundy**
- **Brushes: flat brush, mop**
- **Basic brush loading kit (see page 49)**

1 Use a flat brush to apply a coat of water or retarder mix to the area to be painted.

2 Rinse and moisten the brush as usual. Dip the corner of the brush into the paint and dab the paint into the middle of the damp area.

3 While the paint is still wet, dab a dry mop lightly over the paint to disperse it, working from the outside in.

also see the following pages
Applying the base coat 28–29
Crackle finish 38 • **Transferring a design** 25
Brush loading and brushwork basics 48–49
Side loading 66–71
Liner brushstrokes 62–65
Shading and highlighting 100–107
The final touch 114–117

Project 3

Crackled pansy mirror

This project has always been a favorite with my classes. The subtle colors fit in with so many schemes, and it's a fun way to learn about crackle medium.

YOU WILL NEED

- **Palette: Uniform Blue and Dove Grey base with Avocado, Antique Teal, Light Buttermilk, Moon Yellow, Golden Straw, and Lamp Black**
- **Brushes: wide, flat brush, No. 8 or 10 flat brush, No. 3 or 5 round brush, No. 0 or 1 liner, synthetic brush for varnishing**
- **Basic brush loading kit (see page 49)**
- **Brush 'n' Blend blending medium**
- **Sealed square mirror with a wide frame**
- **Fine-grade sandpaper**
- **Crackle medium**
- **Natural sponge**
- **Pansy motif**
- **Tracing paper**
- **Masking tape**
- **Transfer paper**
- **Stylus**
- **Matte varnish**

1 Use a wide flat brush to apply a Uniform Blue base coat to the sealed mirror frame. Dry, sand, and repeat. Leave to dry completely.

2 Decide which areas of the mirror will be covered by the design. Rinse the wide brush and apply a coat of crackle medium to the frame, avoiding the sections to be painted later. Leave to dry completely.

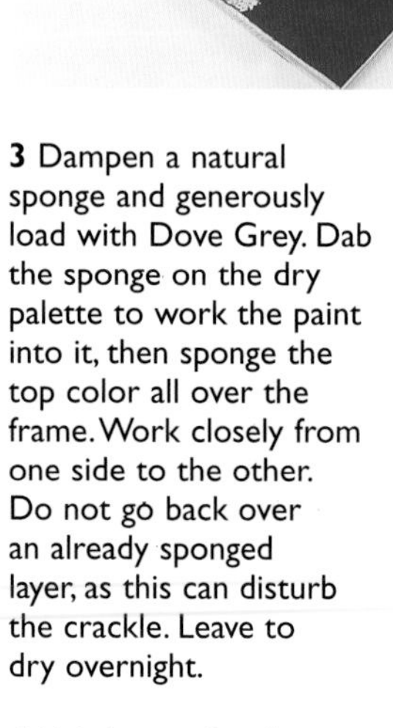

3 Dampen a natural sponge and generously load with Dove Grey. Dab the sponge on the dry palette to work the paint into it, then sponge the top color all over the frame. Work closely from one side to the other. Do not go back over an already sponged layer, as this can disturb the crackle. Leave to dry overnight.

4 Lightly transfer the pansy motif to the frame.

5 Load a flat brush with Avocado, fill in the leaves, and leave to dry. Repeat, and dry again.

6 Rinse the flat brush and side load with Antique Teal. Use to add areas of shade to the leaves. Leave to dry.

7 Load a liner with Antique Teal and paint in the veins.

The crackle effect gives the aged appearance of an object well-loved.

8 Load a small amount of Light Buttermilk onto a dry round brush and rub off excess paint on a paper towel. Use this to apply a highlight to each leaf. (See Dry-brush highlighting, page 106.)

9 Apply a layer of blending medium with a clean flat brush to the flowers. Side load a clean flat brush with Uniform Blue and shade around the edges of each petal. Leave to dry.

10 Apply another layer of blending medium and fully load a round brush with Moon Yellow. Pull the brush from the center out to the edges of the petals, but not over the blue. Leave to dry.

11 Rinse and reload the round brush with a little Golden Straw, and again work from the center to the edges of each petal, without touching the blue. Leave to dry.

12 Side load the flat brush with Uniform Blue and shade where the outer edges of the petals meet other petals.

13 Rinse and side load with Light Buttermilk. Highlight the top edges of the petals.

14 Use the liner loaded with Lamp Black to paint in the center of the flowers and the "whiskers." Leave to dry.

The finished mirror would make a pretty accent in a bathroom or hallway. The color of the pansies could easily be changed, if necessary, to complement the decor.

15 Rinse the liner and use it to add a tiny "C" stroke of Golden Straw to each flower center.

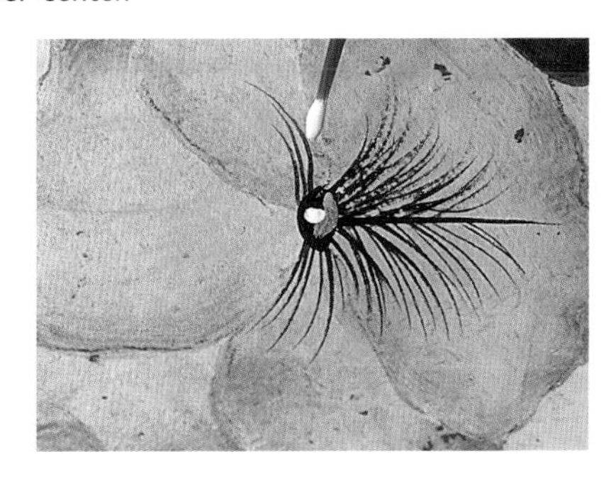

16 Rinse the liner and finish each flower center with a dot of Light Buttermilk.

17 Rinse the liner and load with Avocado. Add the tendrils.

18 Leave for 24 hours and finish with several coats of matte varnish.

SHAPE, FORM AND DESIGN

SHAPE, FORM, AND DESIGN

Choosing the most appropriate form of shading or highlighting will allow your paintings to appear more life-like, and decorative borders can add shape and form to a whole design. Of course, you will want to preserve your masterpeice with the correct finish!

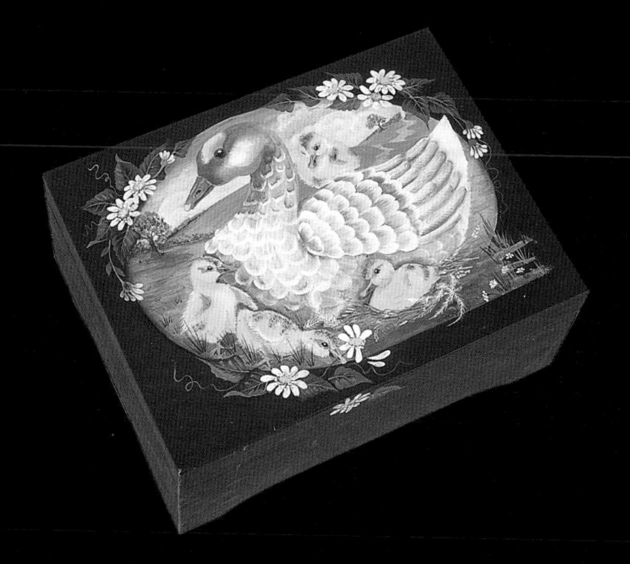

Shading and highlighting

The simplest of folk and decorative art offers flat shapes that give an impression of the subject. For example, a red circle could be a cherry, and a red crescent a tulip. To give your painting the illusion of shape, you can add dimension by using shading and highlighting.

The goose feathers are detailed with a side-loaded brush, and the border is broken with round-brush daisies.

The light source

The most important point to consider when shading and highlighting is the position of the light source. Draw a small arrow or sun in pencil or chalk (which can be erased later) on the surface to show you the direction the light is coming from. In the examples on these pages, the light source is coming from the top right. Knowing exactly where your light source is will allow you to clearly see where highlighted areas should be—the highest point facing the light source—and where the darkest areas are—furthest away from the light source or obstructed from it. Both the light and dark areas will diffuse into the middle area and will need to be graduated across the design.

Here a liner brush is used to add detailed highlights.

Reverse highlighting

The finishing touch to your shape is the reverse highlight. With the light source in the top right-hand corner of the design, some light will miss the object and hit an object or area beyond. This will reflect the light back toward your shapes. This reflection of light is always on the opposite side of the object to the light source and is called a reverse highlight.

In the apricots below I have used Jade Green to add reverse highlights. Of course the color would vary depending on what the light was being reflected from and to.

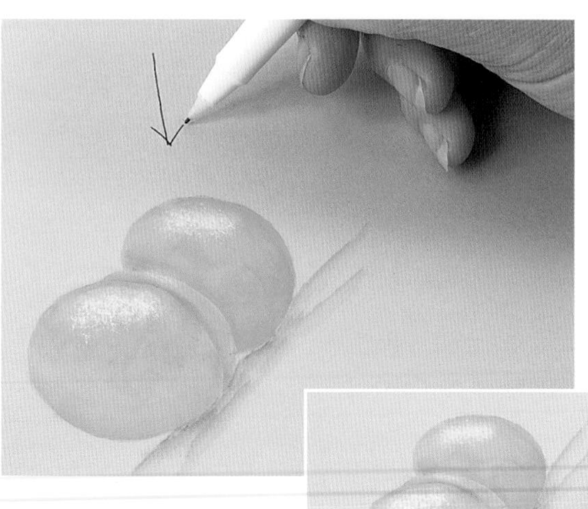

1 Mark the direction of the light source, and then an arrow opposite to denote the direction of the reverse highlight.

Different shapes painted in similar shades give cohesion to this design of Christmas roses, aconite, and oak.

The examples given in this section of the book will help you practice the basic techniques. Once you have mastered them, you will find it easy to transfer these skills to painting other shaped objects.

2 Side load a flat brush with Jade Green, and add the reverse highlight.

Light source practice grapes

For the first practice I have outlined a bunch of grapes to demonstrate that even if a shape is facing the light source, if it is covered by another object it will be dark or shaded.

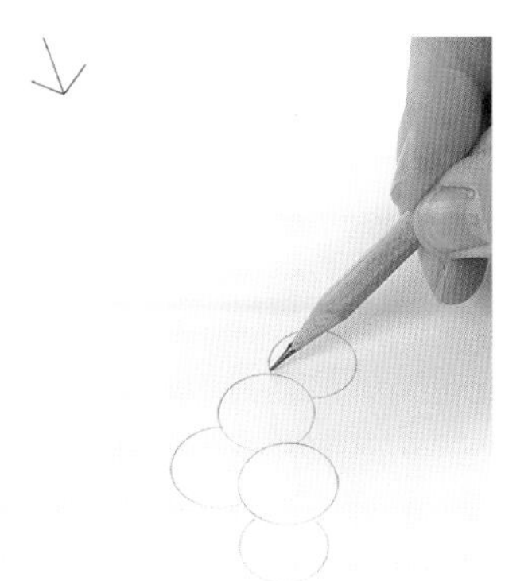

1 Draw the basic outline of your grapes, remembering that some will overlap each other. Then add an arrow, indicating where your light source is coming from.

2 Where grapes overlap each other, the light source is obstructed, so shade these areas.

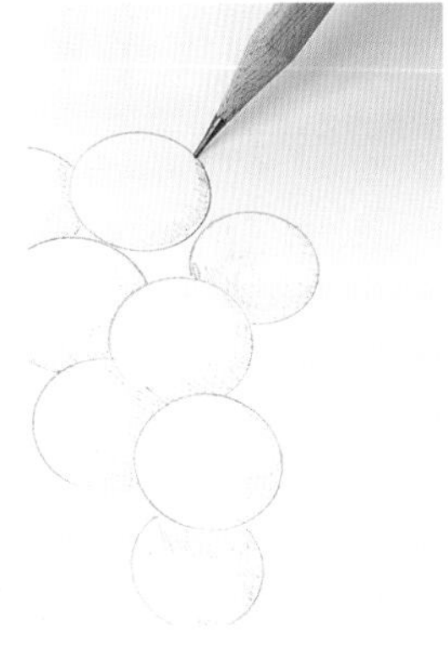

3 Shade areas that are facing away from the light source.

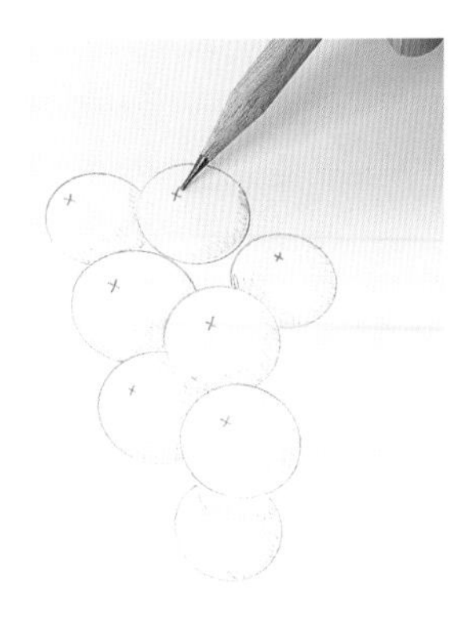

4 Now the shading is complete. To add highlights, indicate the point where the light source hits each grape.

A smoked grey background makes an ideal base for a softly painted posy of violets.

Wet blending

For a very gradual transition in color, wet blending is an effective technique. Applying a coat of blending medium before painting your shape will enable you to move your paint for quite a long time.

YOU WILL NEED

- **Palette: Silver Sage Green base, Violet Haze, and Titanium White**
- **Brushes: round brush**
- **Basic brush loading kit (see page 49)**

1 First apply a coat of retarder mix to the area to be painted.

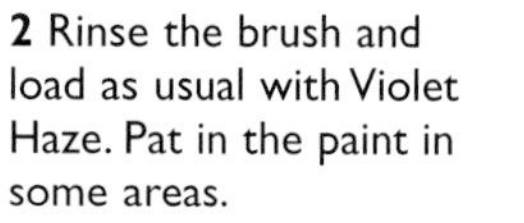

2 Rinse the brush and load as usual with Violet Haze. Pat in the paint in some areas.

3 Rinse the brush again and load the damp brush with Titanium White. Pat in the paint in the areas adjacent to the Violet Haze.

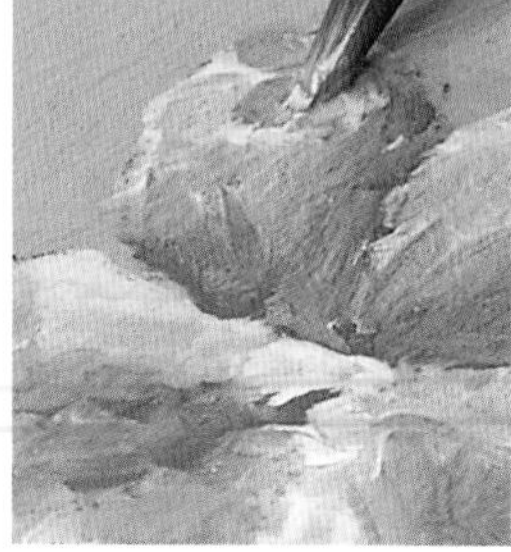

4 Rinse the brush and pull strokes through the two colors, lightly skimming the surface.

5 Continue until the two colors fade into each other.

LEFT *Painting glassware is always a challenge; consideration must be given not only to the light source, but the way in which light reflects on the glass itself, and is bounced off again.*

RIGHT *Dots and linerwork highlight the different shaped elements of this mix of berries, wheat and poppy.*

Dot-and-dash highlighting

On some objects, especially shiny ones, the final highlight can be quite strong, but very small in relation to its size. A single dot, a group of dots, or tiny commas give the final touch of light.

A highlight is given to this leaf with a short line at the highest point of its center vein.

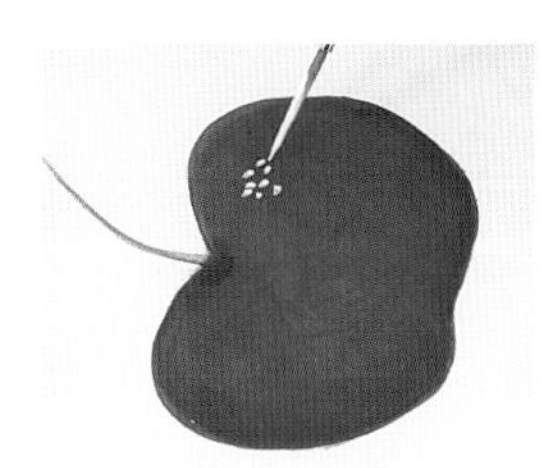

A group of tiny dots gives shine to a cherry.

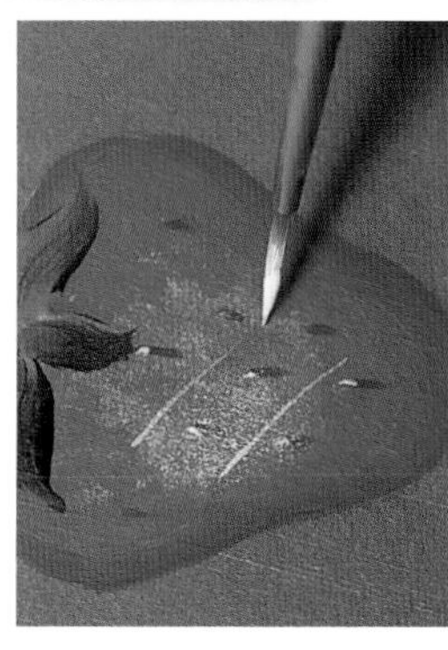

Fine line crosshatching denotes several highlit areas in close proximity, adding texture to the strawberry.

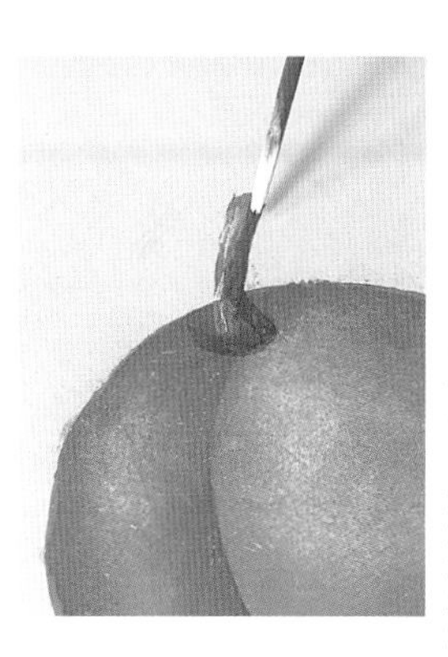

A tiny dash highlight is sufficient on this stalk.

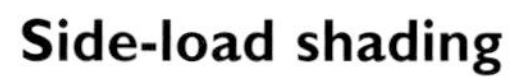

Shading

Using the side loading techniques detailed in Essential Strokes (see pages 66–71) over a damp or retarded base gives you longer to perfect your shading. (See also The light source, page 100.)

Side-load shading

Side loading is an excellent way of changing the shape of an object by adding layers of darker colors. Dampening the base with water or a retarder mix will make it easier to achieve an even transition of color, and the paint is best picked up with a moist brush.

YOU WILL NEED

- **Palette: Violet Haze and Diox Purple**
- **Brushes: No. 10 flat or angle brush**
- **Basic brush loading kit (see page 49)**
- **Water or Brush 'n' Blend blending medium**

1 Load a flat brush with Violet Haze, and paint the basic shape of your plum. Leave to dry.

2 Dampen the whole area across the plum and beyond its edges with water or blending medium.

3 Side load a flat brush with Diox Purple, and shade around the shape. Leave to dry, then dampen again and shade the crease.

Side-loaded highlights and shading give shape to the ruddy cheeks and chin of this beaming sun.

Highlighting

When you are highlighting it is important to think about the texture of your object. Is it smooth and shiny, velvety (like a peach), or slightly textured? The amount of blending, particularly with mopped or dry-brush highlights, will determine the texture you achieve in your finish. (See also The light source, page 100.)

Side-load highlighting

This technique is used where a light area is against a hard edge.

YOU WILL NEED

- **Palette: Deep Periwinkle Blue, Admiral Blue, Light Buttermilk**
- **Brushes: flat or angle brush**
- **Basic brush loading kit (see page 49)**

1 Moisten a flat or angle brush in the retarder mix and dab off the excess onto a paper towel.

2 Pick up paint on one corner and blend on the wet palette. The color should be strong on the corner and fade to nothing across the brush.

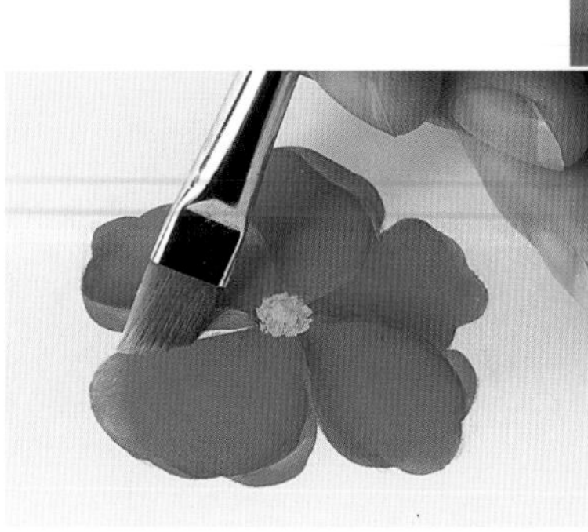

3 Apply to the surface, fading the ends of the float with the clean side of the brush.

Shaded and highlighted shell

This shell project uses shading and highlighting to build the shape completely: there is no basic painted shape that is shaded and highlighted over the top. The shape relies on decreasing areas of shading and then highlighting to make it appear curved and shiny.

YOU WILL NEED

- **Palette: Buttermilk base with Khaki Tan, Mississippi Mud, Burnt Sienna, Burnt Umber, Light Buttermilk, and Titanium White**
- **Brushes: No. 10 flat or ¼-inch (0.5cm) angle brush, No. 2 round brush, No. 1 liner, mop**
- **Basic brush loading kit (see page 49)**
- **Brush 'n' Blend blending medium**
- **Motif, tracing paper, masking tape, transfer paper, and stylus (optional)**

1 Either paint freehand or transfer the design to the prepared and base-coated surface (see page 25).

2 Moisten the flat or angle brush, and side load with Khaki Tan, aiming for quite a wide load. Shade around the outside edge and the inside curve of the shell shape. Leave to dry.

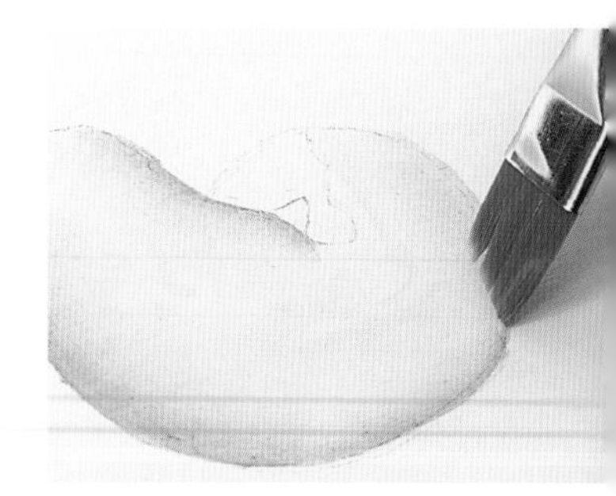

3 Remoisten the brush and pick up a narrower side load of Mississippi Mud. Shade over the same area and leave to dry.

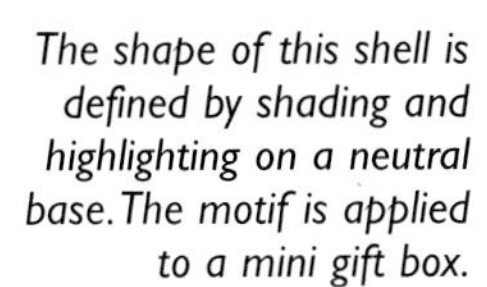

The shape of this shell is defined by shading and highlighting on a neutral base. The motif is applied to a mini gift box.

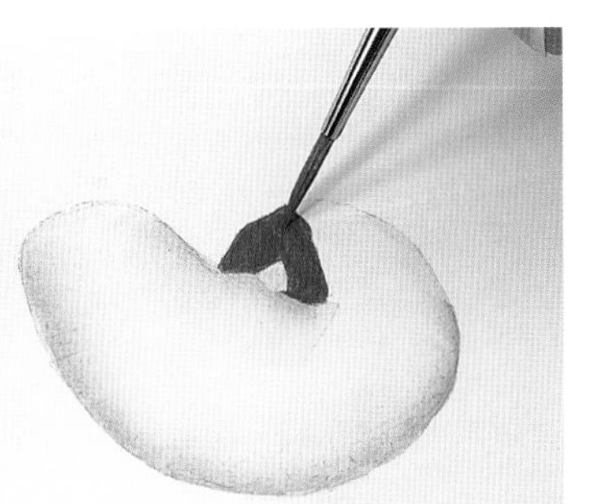

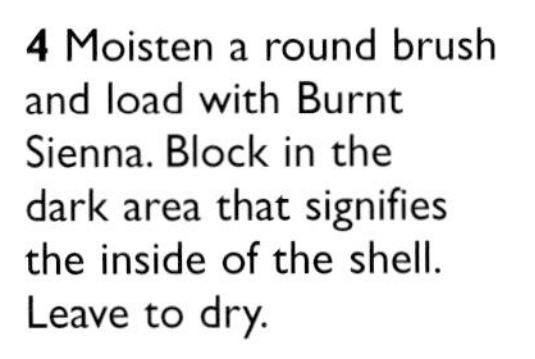

4 Moisten a round brush and load with Burnt Sienna. Block in the dark area that signifies the inside of the shell. Leave to dry.

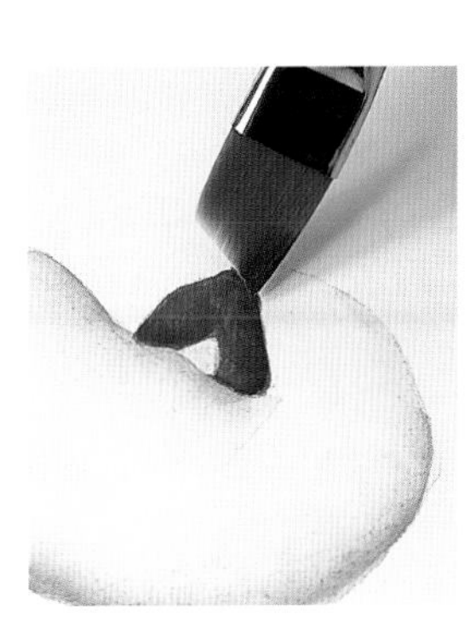

5 Moisten the flat or angle brush, side load with Burnt Umber and shade the outside edges of the Burnt Sienna block.

6 Load a liner with Burnt Sienna, and pull out fine lines around the central curve (see page 62).

7 Use the same brush and color with pressured strokes to fill in the other details (see page 64).

8 Dampen the areas to be highlighted with blending medium or water. Moisten the flat or angle brush and highlight the raised areas of the shell using back-to-back floats (see page 70) in Light Buttermilk. Leave to dry.

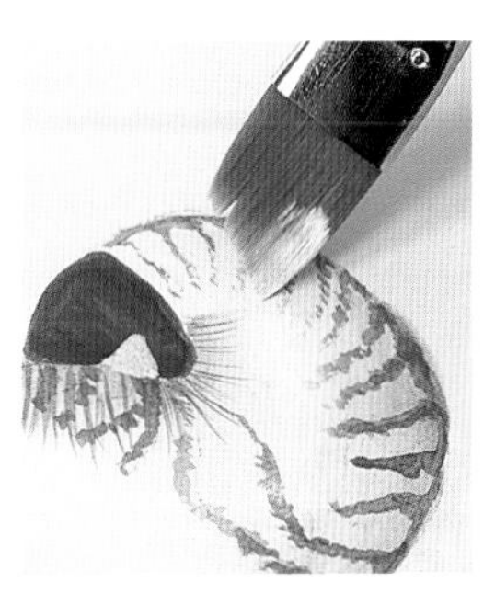

9 Repeat step 8 with Titanium White over a smaller area.

10 While the Titanium White is still damp, use a dry mop to soften the edges.

This vibrant Zhostovo placemat is finished with a gold linerwork border. Here, rather unusually, the light source is coming from directly above, causing the center of the design to be much brighter than the outer areas.

Mopped or layered highlighting

YOU WILL NEED

- **Palette: Country Red and Titanium White**
- **Brushes: flat brush, mop**
- **Basic brush loading kit (see page 49)**
- **Brush 'n' Blend blending medium**

1 Use a flat brush to apply a coat of water or blending medium to a wider area than needs to be highlighted.

2 Rinse and moisten the brush as usual. Dip the corner of the brush into the paint and dab the paint into the middle of the damp area.

3 Gently work a dry mop over the still-wet paint until the edges fade away. Allow to dry.

4 Repeat steps 2–3 over the already mopped highlight, but across a smaller area to increase the "height."

Dry-brush highlighting

This is a very soft highlight that is built up gradually by brushing on more color or adding a lighter color.

YOU WILL NEED

- **Palette: Medium Flesh and Titanium White**
- **Brushes: stippler**
- **Basic brush loading kit (see page 49)**

1 Take a dry stippler and dip it in a little light-colored paint.

2 Work the paint into the brush on a dry palette.

3 Dab the brush on a paper towel until most of the paint is removed.

4 Test the paint load by brushing on a dark surface, you should barely be able to see the color.

5 Hold the brush vertically and dab the bristles evenly over the surface. The color will gradually come off the brush and build up to a subtle highlight.

Shaded and highlighted pear

YOU WILL NEED

- **Palette: Moon Yellow, Golden Straw, Antique Gold, Raw Umber, Light Buttermilk, Sable Brown, Deep Burgundy, Titanium White**
- **Brushes: No, 10 & No.6 flat brush or ¼-inch angle shader, mop, liner**
- **Basic brush loading kit (see page 49)**
- **Brush 'n' Blend blending medium**
- **Motif, tracing paper, masking tape, transfer paper, and stylus**

1 Transfer the design lightly onto your prepared base (see page 25). Base the pear with Moon Yellow. Leave to dry, then repeat.

A shallow tote with high ends is decorated with pieces of fruit and a checkered edge.

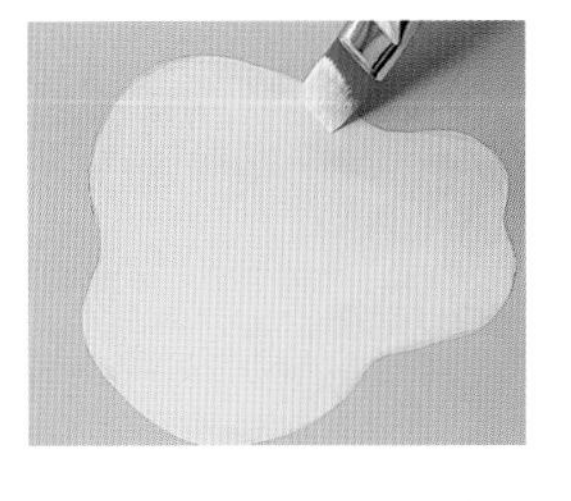

2 Dampen the whole area across the pear and beyond its edges with water or Brush 'n' Blend. Side load a No.10 flat brush with Golden Straw, and shade around the edges of the pear. Dry.

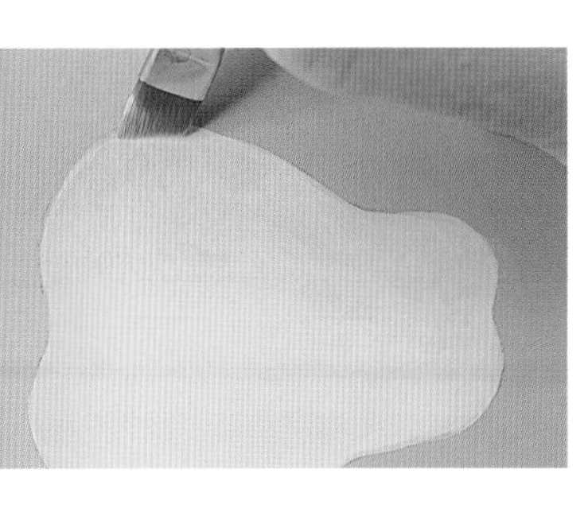

3 Dampen the area again with water or blending medium. With a narrower side load (using the No. 6 flat brush or angle shader), deepen the shading around the bottom of the pear, fading it into the sides so there are no hard lines. Also shade the "dips." Leave to dry.

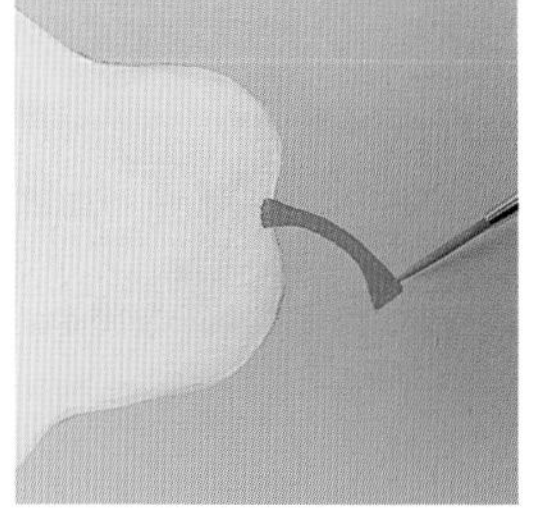

4 Load the liner brush with Sable Brown and paint in the stalk. Leave to dry.

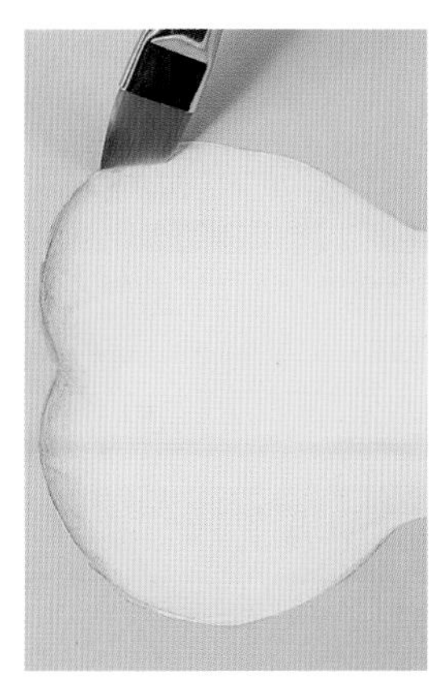

5 Dampen the bottom area with water or blending medium. Shade the very bottom and the dip for the stalk with a side load of Raw Umber.

6 Load a flat brush with Titanium White. Dampen the right-hand half and dot some Light Buttermilk into the "fat" areas. Before it dries, use a dry mop to blend the light areas so they fade at the edges. Leave to dry.

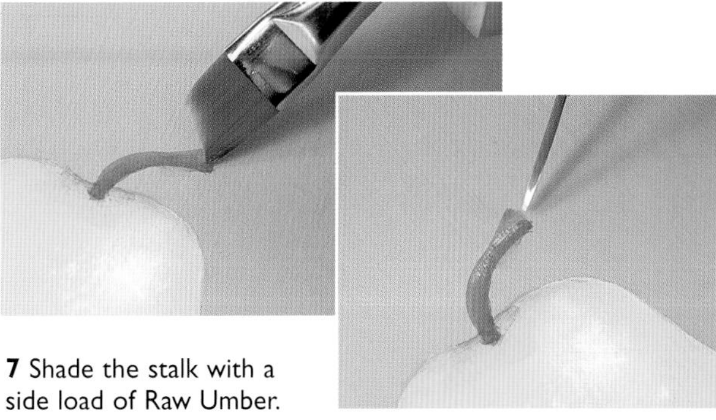

7 Shade the stalk with a side load of Raw Umber.

8 Dry brush a tiny highlight with Light Buttermilk.

Shaped surfaces

Some designs rely on shape to give them interest. Lumps and bumps catch light and create shade. You can create this illusion using the highlighting and shading techniques you have already learned. Think about the shape of the object you are depicting and the parts that are nearest to you. Which parts catch the most light and which are in the deepest shade?

Basketwork

This close-up example of basketwork shows how you can change a flat surface into a very shapely one using one shading and one highlighting technique.

YOU WILL NEED

- **Palette: Raw Sienna, Burnt Umber, and Antique White**
- **Brushes: No 10 flat brush, No 1 liner, ¼-inch (0.5cm) stippler or deerfoot**
- **Basic brush loading kit (see page 49)**
- **Pencil**

1 Lightly mark the area to be painted with a rough brickwork pattern.

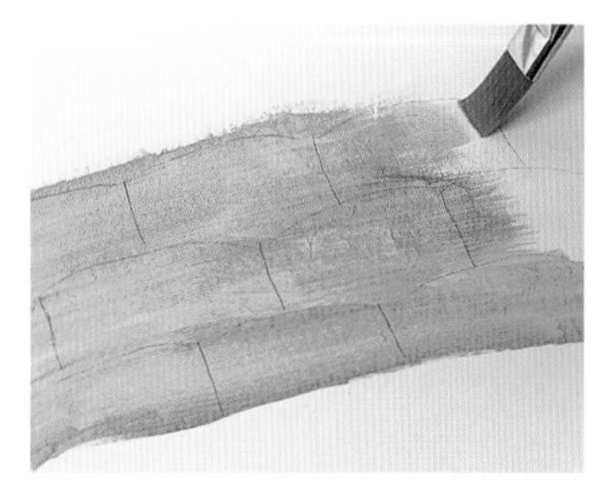

2 Load a flat brush with the Raw Sienna as normal and lightly paint over the pencil lines. Leave to dry.

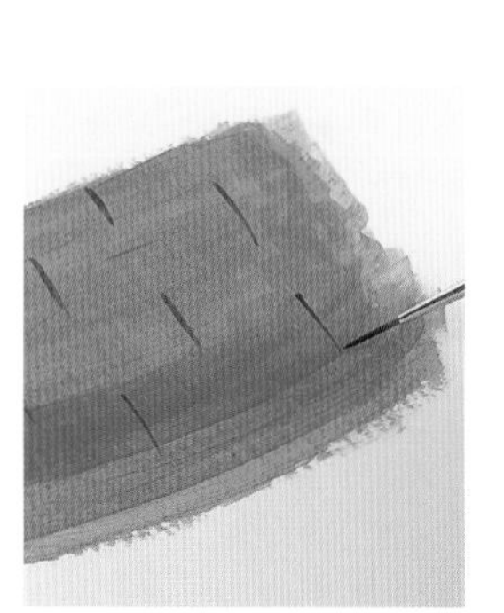

3 Load a liner with thinned Burnt Umber and paint in the upright lines over your pencil marks (see pages 62–65). Leave to dry.

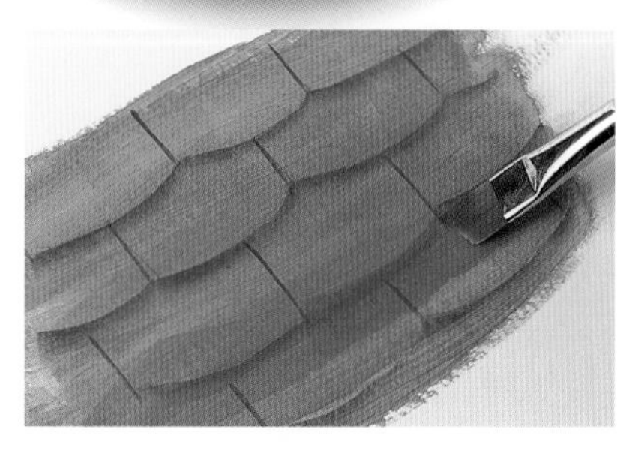

4 Moisten the flat brush, side load with Burnt Umber, and shade under the curves between the vertical lines (see page 100). Don't worry if the result is slightly irregular, it is more realistic that way.

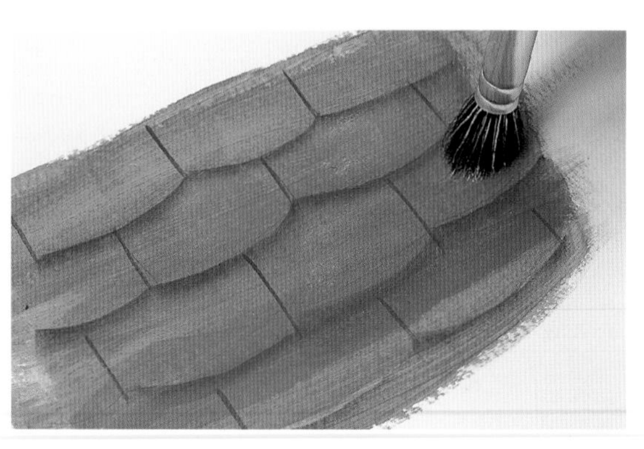

5 Pick up some Antique White on a dry stippler or deerfoot and highlight the "fattest" parts of the overlapping bands (see page 106).

LEFT A decorative plate with all the ingredients for ratatouille—the shapes are developed with layers of shading and highlighting.

RIGHT A pretty hanging sign shows a wicker basket filled with stippled flowers.

Basket of flowers

YOU WILL NEED

- **Palette: Yellow Ochre base and Raw Sienna, Burnt Umber, Antique White, Admiral Blue, Country Blue, Titanium White, and Hauser Medium Green**
- **Brushes: No. 3 round brush, No. 1 liner, No. 4 flat or ¼-inch (0.5cm) angle brush, No. 4 stippler**
- **Basic brush loading kit (see page 49)**
- **Motif, tracing paper, masking tape, transfer paper, and stylus**

1 Lightly transfer the main pattern lines of the basket motif to the surface (see page 25).

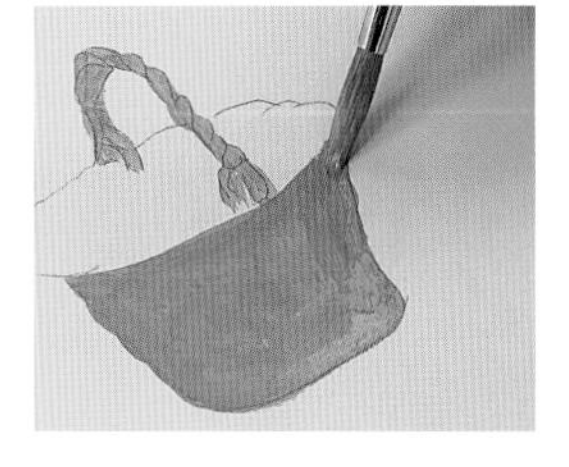

2 Load a round brush with Raw Sienna as normal and lightly paint over the pencil lines. Leave to dry.

3 Now lightly transfer the basketwork detail over the dry painted base.

4 Use a liner to paint in the vertical lines with Burnt Umber. Leave to dry.

5 Moisten the flat or angle brush. Side load with more Burnt Umber, and shade under the curves between the vertical lines.

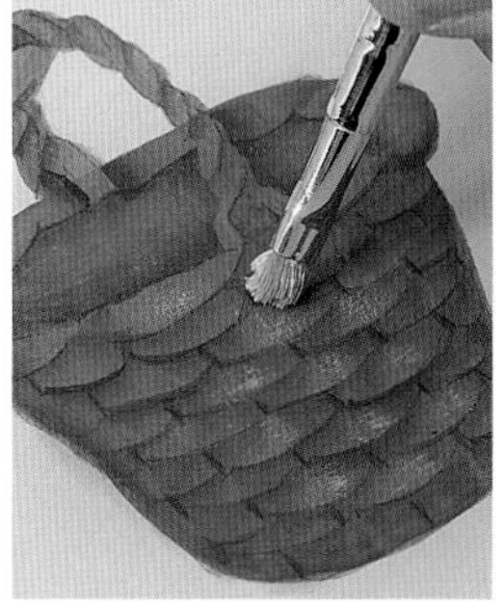

6 Pick up a little Antique White on a dry stippler and highlight the "fattest" parts of the overlapping bands.

7 Stipple (see page 86) in the flowers using Admiral Blue, Country Blue, and Titanium White.

8 Rinse the liner and use long comma strokes (see page 64) to paint the leaves in with Hauser Medium Green.

Enhancements

A plate with a central design of fruit edged with checks and cherries.

The extra touches can really add to your painted design. A border, for example, can make all the difference to your finished piece. You can mask off the edge of your piece and apply a paint finish, reusing some of the colors in the design (see pages 32–39), or, by grouping together some simple strokes, you can design your own border very easily. Quick little hearts can be used on their own or in a border. I have used Hauser

Curved commas and dots border

YOU WILL NEED

- **Palette: Hauser Dark Green and Country Red**
- **Brushes: round brush**
- **Basic brush loading kit (see page 49)**
- **Ruler, pencil, and eraser**
- **Stylus**

1 Use a ruler and pencil to lightly mark a guideline to weave the border motif around.

2 Load a round brush with Hauser Dark Green. Paint curved commas (see page 50) under and over the line.

3 Dip a stylus in the Country Red and use it to add dots on the line, between each comma. You will need to reload for each dot. Leave to dry.

4 When you are sure the paint is absolutely dry, carefully erase the pencil line.

Straight commas and dots border

YOU WILL NEED

- **Palette: Country Red and Hauser Dark Green**
- **Brushes: round brush**
- **Basic brush loading kit (see page 49)**
- **Ruler, pencil, and eraser**
- **Stylus**

1 Use a ruler and pencil to lightly mark a guideline to base the border along.

2 Load a round brush with Hauser Dark Green. Paint straight commas (see page 50) evenly spaced along the line.

Fine line and dot border

YOU WILL NEED

- **Palette: Hauser Dark Green and Country Red**
- **Brushes: No 1 liner**
- **Basic brush loading kit (see page 49)**
- **Ruler, pencil, and eraser**
- **Stylus**

1 Use a ruler and pencil to lightly mark a guideline to base the border along.

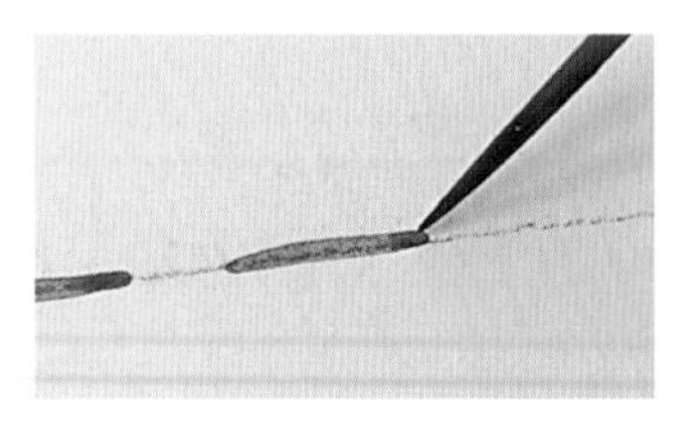

2 Load a liner with the first color and paint short fine lines, evenly spaced along the line (see page 62).

Dark Green and Country Red in the following demonstrations, but I would suggest you choose colors you have already used in your design to bring the whole piece together. Alternatively, on a dark background, gold can look absolutely stunning.

A single line of checks can be used to enhance a plain edge, or add several rows to make a structured border. The width of your brush will dictate the width of the checks, so use one that is slightly smaller than the space

RIGHT *Gold and white linerwork make a lovely frame for a pretty lady.*

3 Dip a stylus in the Country Red and use it to add a dot on the line between each comma. You will need to reload for each dot. Leave to dry.

4 When you are sure the paint is absolutely dry, carefully erase the pencil line.

3 Dip a stylus in the second color and use it to add one dot above and below the line between each fine line. You will need to reload for each dot. Leave to dry.

4 When you are sure the paint is absolutely dry, carefully erase the pencil line.

Fleur-de-lis and dot border

YOU WILL NEED

- **Palette: Country Red and Hauser Dark Green**
- **Brushes: round brush**
- **Basic brush loading kit (see page 49)**
- **Ruler, pencil, and eraser**
- **Stylus**

1 Use a ruler and pencil to lightly mark a guideline to base the border along.

2 Load a round brush with the first color. Paint three curved commas (see page 50) to make a rough fleur-de-lis shape, on its side. Continue to paint the shapes along the line, evenly spaced.

3 Dip a stylus in the second color and use it to add three dots along the line between each fleur-de-lis. You will need to reload for each dot. Leave to dry.

4 When the paint is absolutely dry, carefully erase the pencil line.

Triangle dot border

YOU WILL NEED

- **Palette: Country Red and Hauser Dark Green**
- **Ruler, pencil, and eraser**
- **Stylus**

1 Use a ruler and pencil to lightly mark a guideline to base the border along.

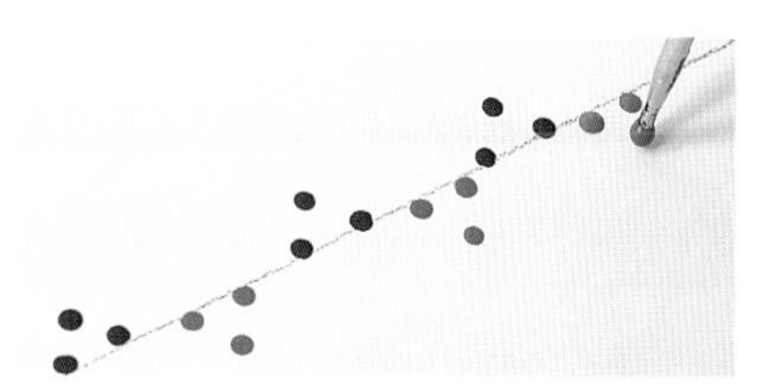

2 Dip a stylus in the first color and paint dots in triangular groups of three, evenly spaced below the line. You will need to reload for each dot.

3 Dip the stylus in the second color and add three dots in a triangular group above the line, between the red dots.

4 When the paint is completely dry, carefully erase the pencil line.

you want to fill. Alternatively, a narrow edge can be enhanced with a solid edging line in a color used in the design, or using gold.

In the speckling technique, random dots of thinned paint are applied to the surface to create a speckled effect. It can be extremely messy, so wear old clothes and protect the area surrounding your piece with plastic sheeting or newspaper. An old toothbrush is ideal for speckling, or Loew Cornell make a speckling brush especially for the purpose.

A simple checkered edge finishes off this wall-mounted container, perfect for a child's room.

Mini hearts

YOU WILL NEED

- **Palette: Country Red**
- **Brushes: any brush with a flat-ended handle, liner**
- **Basic brush loading kit (see page 49)**
- **Paper towel**

1 Mix some paint with a little water on the wet palette to thin it slightly. It should slowly drip off the end of a paintbrush.

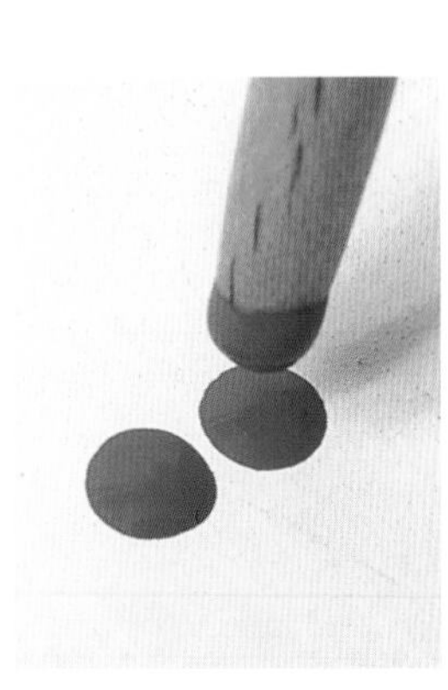

2 Dip the handle end of a brush in the thinned paint. Touch the surface with the handle twice, to make two dots next to each other.

3 Moisten a liner slightly. Touch the bristle tip of the liner in one of the paint dots and pull down in a diagonal line that stops directly under the point where the dots meet. Repeat on the other side, from the other paint dot, and pull a short line between the two dots.

4 Lightly pull the paint into the empty areas in the center of the heart.

5 To elongate the heart, pull longer lines at step 3.

Checkered edges

YOU WILL NEED

- **Palette: Country Red and Hauser Dark Green**
- **Brushes: flat brush**
- **Basic brush loading kit (see page 49)**
- **Ruler, pencil, and eraser**

1 Use a ruler and pencil to lightly mark parallel lines to position the checks inside.

2 Load a flat brush with Country Red. Hold the brush at right angles to the surface and, starting on the top line, pull down to meet the bottom line, applying very slight pressure. At the bottom line, let the bristles straighten before lifting the brush off.

3 Paint the next stroke in the same way, one brush-width away from the previous stroke. When complete, leave to dry.

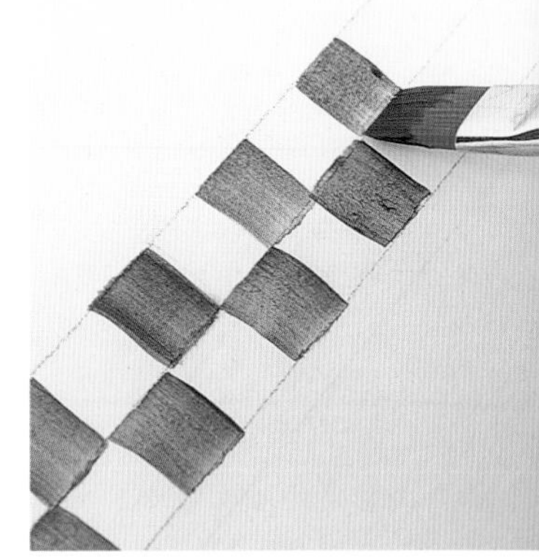

4 Alternatively, draw three parallel lines and paint alternate squares between each pair of lines, for a double check. When complete, leave to dry.

5 When you are sure the paint is absolutely dry, carefully erase the pencil lines.

Posies of pale violets adorn each side of this trinket box, with a smoked marble finish.

Solid edge

YOU WILL NEED

- **Palette: Gold**
- **Brushes: flat brush**
- **Basic brush loading kit (see page 49)**
- **Gold marker pen**

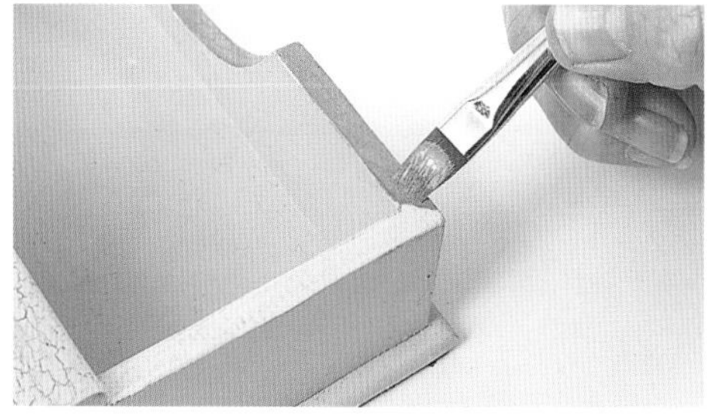

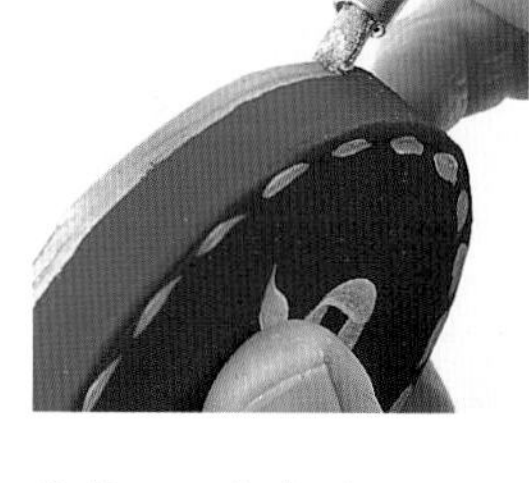

1 Load a flat brush with Gold paint. Hold the brush parallel to the top of the edge being painted.

2 Pull the side of the brush along the edge to apply the paint, exerting only light pressure. This allows you to paint the edge without excess paint spilling over the sides.

3 Alternatively, draw along an edge with a gold marker pen.

Speckling

YOU WILL NEED

- **Palette: Raw Umber**
- **Brushes: flat brush, speckling brush or an old toothbrush, and another brush handle**
- **Wet palette**
- **Paper towel**

1 On a wet palette, make a puddle of Raw Umber, thinned with water so that it looks like tinted water.

2 Roll a speckling brush or dip an old toothbrush in the thinned paint. Tap the brush on a paper towel to knock off excess paint.

3 Hold the speckling brush firmly in one hand about 6–12 inches (15–30cm) above your surface. Twist the handle with the other hand and the metal pin will rub against the bristles, dispersing the paint across the surface in a fine spray of dots.

4 If using the toothbrush, hold it a similar distance from the surface with the bristles down and pull another brush handle across the bristles to release the paint in a fine spray of dots.

The final touch

A spray of primroses and a generous bee are painted on this tea light holder.

When you have spent so much time and effort preparing and painting your piece, you will, of course, want to preserve it in a pristine condition. The most effective way of doing this is by varnishing. Several coats of a good quality varnish will give your piece a solid protective layer that will withstand knocks and (some) spills. If your piece is a "working" object, such as a tray, extra layers of varnish will be needed to give it a practical finish. Choose your varnish carefully. In the case of

Basic finishing

YOU WILL NEED

- **Brushes: synthetic brush**
- **Eraser**
- **Brown paper bag**
- **Lint-free cloth or tack cloth**
- **Varnish**
- **Old spoon or stirring implement**
- **Shallow glass or plastic dish**
- **Fine wet-and-dry sandpaper**

1 Leave your project to cure for at least 24 hours before starting to varnish.

2 Carefully erase any remaining pattern lines.

3 Smooth the surface by rubbing all over with a brown paper bag—there is just enough roughness in the paper to take out any little rough areas.

4 Lightly wipe all over with a damp, lint-free cloth or tack cloth to remove surface dust. Leave to dry thoroughly.

5 Stir the varnish gently in its container or roll the bottle to ensure the contents are properly mixed. There should be no residue in the bottom. If the bottle is shaken, bubbles appear that can be transferred to your surface and leave an uneven finish.

6 Pour a little varnish into a shallow glass or plastic dish, wider than your brush. This makes it easier to load your brush.

a tray, it will need to be waterproof and heat-resistant. Even so, it is not a good idea to put a hot teapot directly onto a painted tray without a mat underneath.

Having chosen the varnish most suitable for your use, you need to decide how shiny you want the finish to be. Varnishes are available in matte, satin, and gloss finishes, and you may also be able to find "dead flat" varnish that has virtually no sheen at all. Matte varnish is the easiest to apply, as the

A tinted varnish works well with the old-fashioned design and shape of this small chest.

Fluff free

Never wear fluffy clothing when varnishing. The tiny fibers waft around in the air and invariably some will land on your wet surface. If this does happen, wait until the surface is dry but not "set," and gently scratch the fiber free with a fingernail.

7 Dip the brush into the varnish so it is no more than half full. Wipe any excess off on the edge of the dish.

9 Apply a second coat in the same way and leave to dry.

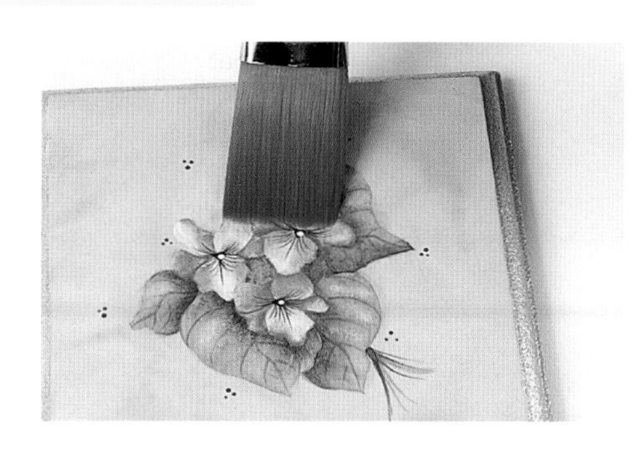

8 Apply the varnish to the surface with even strokes, making sure there are no dribbles down the sides. Allow to dry thoroughly. If you use a hair dryer to speed up the drying, make sure the surface has completely cooled before applying a second coat.

10 Use a very fine wet-and-dry sandpaper to lightly sand the varnished piece. Wipe off the dust with a damp lint-free cloth or tack cloth.

11 You can add more coats, sanding between alternate layers, until you achieve the desired level of protection or find a finish you are happy with.

Groups of acorns and blackberries give an autumnal look to this little shelf.

low sheen does not show up brushstrokes easily. Gloss varnish is the clearest, whereas the less shiny finishes are "dulled" with suspended particles. This can give a slightly cloudy finish over many coats, so if you are intending to varnish your piece many times, it is better to use a gloss for most of the coats, finishing with a couple of coats of a less shiny varnish if you want a flatter finish.

I like to use a wide synthetic brush for varnishing. These are relatively expensive but do give an even coat without brushmarks. Some painters prefer foam or sponge brushes, but these can introduce tiny bubbles to the surface. Whichever you choose, keep it for varnishing only. Do not use it for base coating or paint effects.

Tinted wash

Using a tinted wash before varnishing is just one of the ways you can "age" your piece.

YOU WILL NEED

- **Palette: Raw Umber**
- **Brushes: wide flat brush, synthetic brush**
- **Very fine sandpaper**
- **Easi Float retarder in a tinting dish**
- **Paper towel**
- **Varnish**
- **Shallow glass or plastic dish**
- **Fine wet-and-dry sandpaper**
- **Lint-free cloth or tack cloth**

1 Use very fine sandpaper to rub away a little of the paint from the corners, edges, and other areas of your piece that would naturally wear.

2 In a tinting dish, prepare a thin wash using 1 tbsp (15ml) of clean water, 10 drops of retarder, and a very little Raw Umber.

3 Mix well, and apply the tint to the piece using a wide flat brush. Make sure the rubbed-back areas are colored.

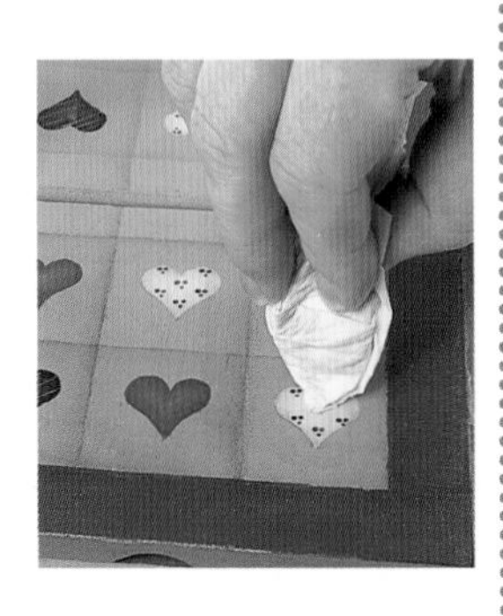

4 Use a paper towel to wipe back areas that are too dark. Leave to completely dry.

5 Continue varnishing in the usual way (see pages 114–115).

Tinted varnishing

You can also use a tinted varnish for the first coat.

YOU WILL NEED

- **Palette: Raw Umber or Burnt Umber**
- **Brushes: synthetic brush**
- **Varnish**
- **Shallow glass or plastic dish**
- **Fine wet-and-dry sandpaper**
- **Lint-free cloth or tack cloth**

1 Pour sufficient varnish to coat your project into a shallow glass or plastic dish.

2 Add a very little Raw or Burnt Umber to the varnish, sufficient just to tint it. Mix well.

3 Test out the tinted varnish on a spare surface before you commit to your finished piece. Remember the varnish needs to still be translucent, and not too dark. To increase translucency and lighten the mix, add more varnish.

4 Apply one coat of tinted varnish as usual (see pages 114–115).

5 Continue finishing with untinted varnish.

Spray varnishes are also available. They must be used in a well-ventilated area, preferably outside, and always wear a mask to avoid inhaling the suspended varnish. To get a good finish you will need to apply many more coats than with a brush varnish.

Decorated with a pastoral scene, this mirror has a textured background and is painted with ochres and dark greens for a "Tuscan" look.

Wax finish

For a professional looking finish you can't beat a wax polish after varnishing. Not only does it add to durability, it somehow changes the resonance of the piece, making it sound more solid.

Make sure the wax polish you purchase does not contain alcohol, as it could damage the painted surface.

YOU WILL NEED

- **Painted and finished piece (see pages 114–115)**
- **Clear wax**
- **Fine wire wool or a worn kitchen scrubber**
- **Soft, lint-free cloth**

1 Leave the varnish on a finished piece to cure for at least three days, preferably longer.

2 Using the wire wool, rub the wax into the surface in a circular motion.

3 Use a soft, lint-free cloth to buff up the wax on the surface to a soft sheen.

Using colored wax

A colored wax can be applied over a varnished surface to give a more aged look than clear wax.

YOU WILL NEED

- **Painted and finished piece (see pages 114–115)**
- **Colored wax**
- **Fine wire wool or a worn kitchen cloth**
- **Soft, lint-free cloth**

1 Leave the varnish on a finished piece to cure for at least three days, preferably longer.

2 Scoop out some colored wax on fine wire wool or a worn kitchen cloth.

3 Using the wire wool, rub the wax into the surface with a circular motion.

4 Use a soft, lint-free cloth to buff up the wax on the surface to a soft sheen.

also see the following pages
Applying the base coat 28–29
Plastic film wrapping 36 • **Masking** 32
Transferring a design 25
Brush loading and brushwork basics 48–49
Side loading 66–71
Shading and highlighting 100–107
Liner brushstrokes 62–65
Enhancements 110–113
The final touch 114–117

Project 4

Geranium tile on a napkin box

This project brings together techniques from each section of this book. The base has a decorative finish, painted and then plastic film wrapped in a complementary color. The top and lower edges are masked off and painted black to give a strong contrast. The design involves creating shape, shading, and highlighting, together with a wash and detailing.

YOU WILL NEED

- **Palette: Raw Sienna base with French Vanilla, Lamp Black, Light Buttermilk, Hauser Medium Green, Hauser Dark Green, Olive Green, Country Red, Black Plum, Coral Rose, Golden Straw, and Gold**
- **Brushes: wide flat brush, No. 1 liner, No. 3 round brush, No 8 filbert, No. 8 flat or ¼-inch (0.5cm) angle brush, synthetic brush for varnishing**
- **Basic brush loading kit (see page 49)**
- **Sealed box (see pages 26–27)**
- **Fine-grade sandpaper**
- **Plastic wrap**
- **Masking tape**
- **Geranium motif**
- **Tracing paper**
- **Transfer paper**
- **Stylus or empty ballpoint pen**
- **Ruler**
- **Waterproof black and gold marker pens**
- **Matte varnish**

1 Sand the sealed box, then use a wide flat brush to apply a Raw Sienna base coat. Dry, and repeat. Leave to dry.

2 Plastic film wrap the outside of the box with French Vanilla.

3 Mask off the bottom edge and a rectangle on the top of the box. Use a liner to paint a thin line of Lamp Black along the edge of the masking tape to further seal the edge and prevent any leakage of the top color. Leave to dry.

4 Rinse the wide flat brush and use to apply a coat of Lamp Black to the top rectangle and bottom edges. Allow to dry and repeat. Leave to dry.

5 Carefully remove the tape.

6 Lightly transfer the geranium motif to the top of the box.

7 Load a round brush with Light Buttermilk and paint in the whole design—if the colors were applied directly over the black they would be muddied by it. Leave to dry.

8 Rinse the brush and load with Hauser Medium Green. Solidly paint in the leaves and calyxes. Dry and repeat. Dry again.

9 Moisten a flat or angle brush and side load with Hauser Dark Green. Shade the veins and edges of the leaves and the calyx edges. Leave to dry.

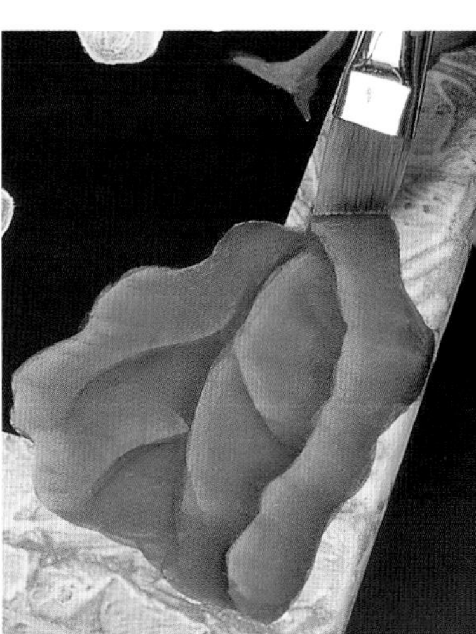

10 Rinse the brush and side load with Olive Green. Use to highlight the leaves and leave to dry.

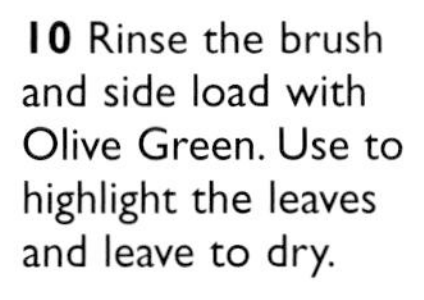

11 Rinse the brush and load as usual with Country Red. Paint a fuzzy stripe well in from the edge of the leaf, but following its shape.

Just the thing for meals outdoors—this striking box will stop your napkins blowing away.

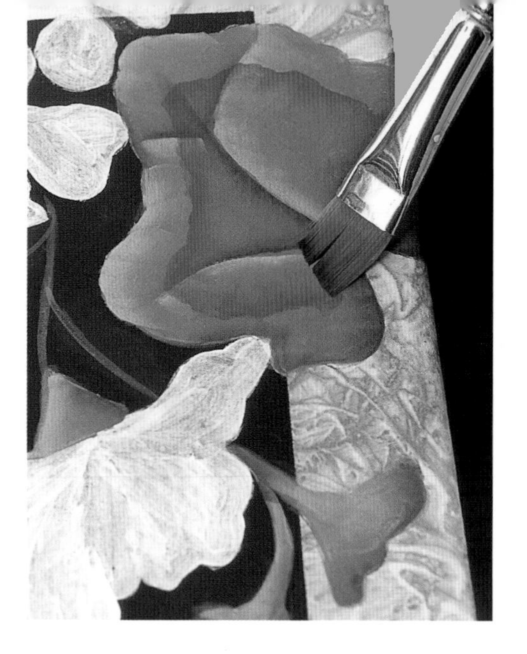

12 Rinse the liner and use it to paint in stalks with a mix of Hauser Medium Green and Olive Green.

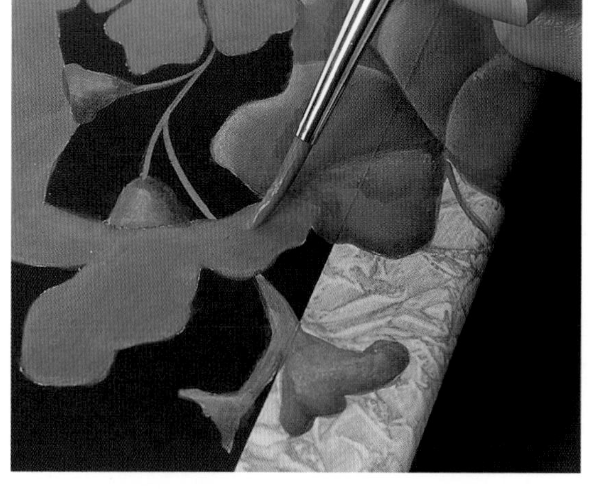

13 Rinse the round brush and use it to paint a solid coat of Country Red on the flowers. Leave to dry, and repeat. Leave to dry again.

14 Rinse the flat or angle brush and side load with Black Plum. Add shadows between the petals and under the turns. Side load again, and float round the centers. Leave to dry.

15 Rinse and side load the flat or angle brush with Coral Rose. Highlight the turns on the petals and light areas of the petals. Subtle is the key. Leave to dry.

16 Rinse the brush and side load with Light Buttermilk. Add highlights in the very middle of some of the already highlighted areas. Leave to dry.

17 Rinse the liner and dot the centers of the flowers with Hauser Medium Green, Golden Straw, and Light Buttermilk.

18 Use a No. 8 flat brush to finish the front edge with gold paint.

20 Use the ruler and a black pen to draw a thin line the same distance outside the rectangle as the gold line is inside it, again, breaking the line where the design overlaps. Use a spray finisher to seal the lines before varnishing.

21 Leave for 24 hours and finish with several coats of matte varnish, inside and out.

This design was inspired by a visit to a tile museum in Shropshire, England, where there is a fascinating display of ceramic tiles from various styles and periods, including art deco and art nouveau.

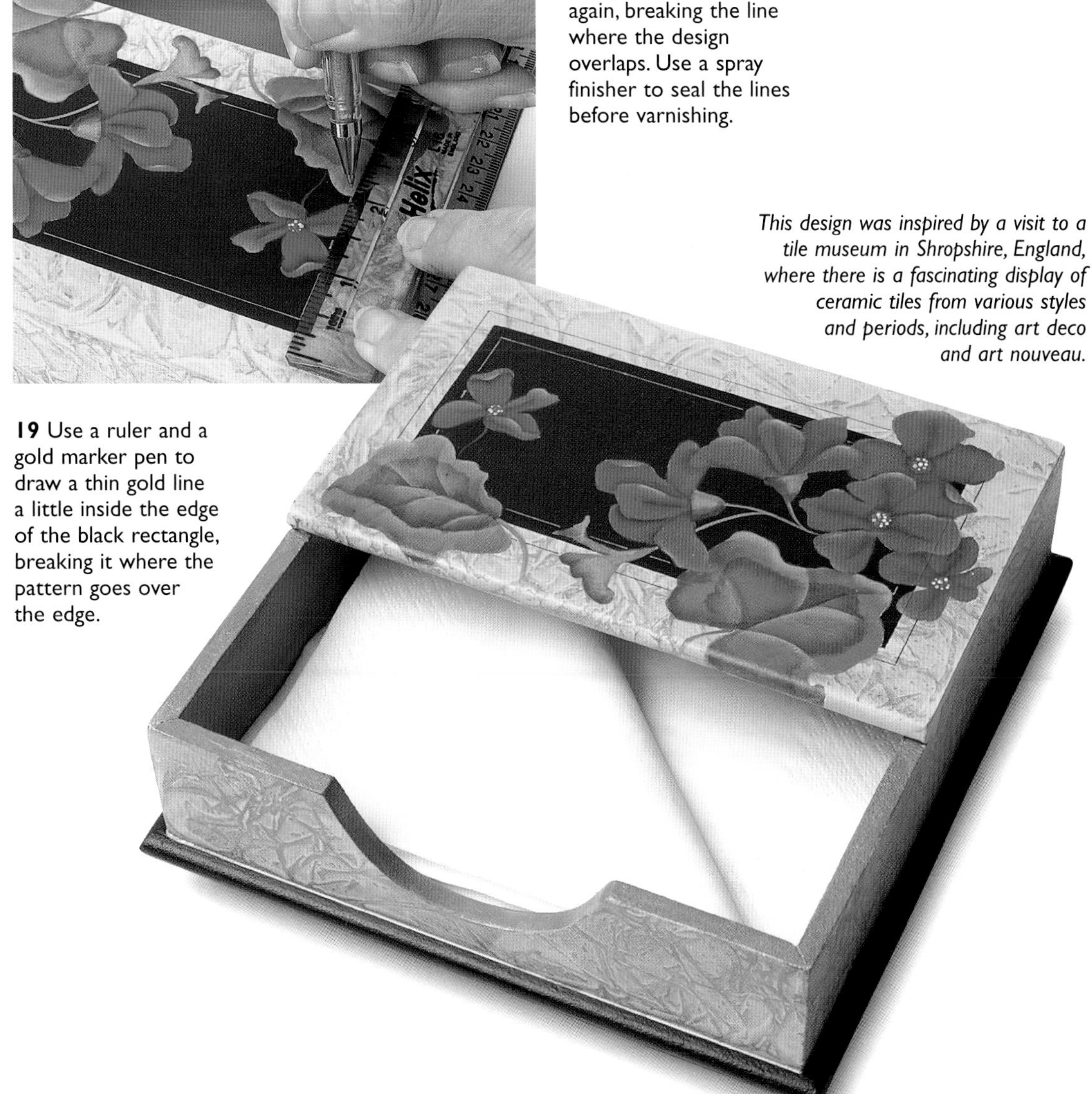

19 Use a ruler and a gold marker pen to draw a thin gold line a little inside the edge of the black rectangle, breaking it where the pattern goes over the edge.

Templates

These templates can be traced onto transfer paper and then onto the surface you wish to paint. Follow the instructions on page 25.

Page 74

Project 2: Daisy and strawberry planter

Page 94

Project 3: Crackled pansy mirror

Page 118

Project 4: Geranium tile on a napkin box

Conversion chart

DecoArt Americana	Delta Ceramicoat	Folk Art
Admiral Blue	Prussian Blue + Purple 1:1	Midnight
Antique Gold	Antique Gold	Yellow Ochre
Antique Rose	Adobe Red	Salmon + Cinnamon 6:1
Antique Teal	Blue Spruce	Teal Green + Wintergreen1:1
Antique White	Trail + White 1:1	Linen
Asphaltum	Burnt Umber	Burnt Sienna + Burnt Umber1:1
Avocado	Seminole Green	Clover
Black Plum	Chocolate Cherry	Burnt Carmine
Blue Mist	Blue Wisp	Summer Sky + Gray Mist 2:1
Burnt Sienna	Burnt Sienna	Burnt Sienna
Burnt Umber	Dark Burnt Umber	Burnt Umber + Burnt Sienna 2:1
Buttermilk	Antique White	Taffy + White 2:1
Coral Rose	Coral	Salmon + Peach Perfection 6:1
Country Blue	Periwinkle Blue	Light Periwinkle
Country Red	Tomato Spice	Red Light + Apple Spice 2:1
Deep Burgundy	Barn Red	True Burgundy
Diox Purple	Purple	Purple
Dove Grey	White + Black 15:1	Light Gray
French Grey Blue	Cape Cod Blue	Settler's Blue
French Vanilla	Flesh Tan	French Vanilla
Golden Straw	Straw	Buttercup
Green Mist	Green Sea + Rainforest (T)	Poetry Green
Hauser Dark Green	Hunter Green	Hunter Green
Hauser Light Green	Lt Foliage Green	Hauser Light Green
Hauser Medium Green	Medium Foliage Green	Hauser Medium Green
Hi Lite Flesh	Pink Frosting	Cotton Candy
Honey Brown	Golden Brown	English Mustard
Jade Green	Wedgwood Green	Bayberry
Khaki Tan	Trail + Sandstone 1:1	Butter Pecan
Lamp Black	Black	Licorice
Light Buttermilk	Light Ivory	Warm White
Light French Blue	Dolphin Grey	Amish Blue
Lilac	White = Lilac 6:1	White + Heather 6:1
Mississippi Mud	Dark Chocolate + Trail 2:1	Coffee Bean + White 3:1
Moon Yellow	Old Parchment	Sunflower + Buttercup 3:1
Olive Green	Leaf Green + White 1:1	Fresh Foliage + Olive (T)
Payne's Grey	Payne's Grey	Payne's Grey + Prussian Blue (T)
Raw Sienna	Raw Sienna	Yellow Light + Terra Cotta 2:1
Raw Umber	Walnut	Raw Umber
Sable Brown	Spice Brown + White 2:1	Teddy Bear Tan + Teddy Bear Br 1:1
Terra Cotta	Raw Sienna + Toffee 3:1	Buckskin Brown
Titanium White	White	Titanium White
Uniform Blue	Cadet Blue	Heartland Blue
Violet Haze	Purple Dusk + Hammered Iron 6:1	Periwinkle + Slate Blue 3:1
Yellow Ochre	Old Parchment + Spice Tan 5:1	Sunflower + Teddy Bear Tan 6:1

Source – TCS Colour Match Source Book
(T) = a touch on color only

Stockists and suppliers

UK

Teachers Forum Trading Company
Westbrook House, Bromham
Chippenham, Wiltshire SN15 2EE
(01380850345 Fax 01380859073)

Books, wood pieces, Loew Cornell brushes, paints, and supplies

Corner House Crafts
Oakleigh
Stour Row Village
Nr Shaftesbury, Dorset
SP7 0QH
(01747838814/5 Fax 01747838080)

DecoArt paints, mediums, varnishes

Art Essentials
26 Main Street
Kimberley, Notts
NG16 2LL

Masterson's Sta-Wet palettes

IKEA
(see local directory for stores)

Unpainted wood pieces

Cottage Designs
Higher Barton, Crow Lane
Ashill,
Ilminster, Somerset
TA19 9LB
di@cottagedesigns.co.uk

Wood pieces

British Association of Decorative & Folk Arts (BADFA)
Membership Secretary
6 Falcon Road
Horndean, Waterlooville, Hants
PO8 9BY

US

Loew-Cornell Inc
563 Chestnut Ave,
Teaneck
NJ 07666
(201-836-7070)

Brushes

DecoArt
PO Box 386
Stanford
KY 40484
(606-365-3193)

Paints, mediums, and varnishes

J.W. ETC
2205 First Street
Suite 103
Simi Valley, CA 93065
(805-526-5066)

Wood filler

IKEA
(see local directory for stores)

Unpainted wood pieces

Tru-Color Systems Inc. (TCS)
64 East Marion Street
PO Box 486
Danville,
Indiana 46122-0486

Society of Decorative Painters
393N McLean Blvd
Wichita,
KS 67203-5968
sdp@southwind.net

Index

Credits

Quarto would like to thank and acknowledge the following for supplying pictures and items reproduced in this book:

(Key: l left, r right, c center, t top, b bottom)

Decorative painters

Ammann, Erika p14b, p27t, p115t (www.erikasfolkart.com)
Belgala, Kathye p50t, p70t, p103tl (kai@netnitco.net)
Bell, Celia p4b, p16t
Bower, Turly p7t, p117t (turlybower@yahoo.com)
Demming, Mary p17t, p28t, p104t, p111t (deming@hrb.de)
Frith, Ghislaine p33t, p110t
Gill, Lola p5t, p8rc, p78-79c, 86t, p93t, p99b, 100t, p101t (lola.gill@cwcom.net)
Harris, Dee p23b, p25t, p29t, p29b, p32t, p34t, p52t, p84t
Harris Peggy p79br, p92t (www.peggyharris.com)
Landwehr, Ellen p6-7c
Rolls, Val p37t, p58t
Sallehudin, Rohaizan p98, p106t (rohaizan@zarada.co.uk)
Stone, Sally p4t, 19t, 26t, p82t (sally@decorativefolkart.co.uk)
Stodgill, Peggy p5b, p8t, 59tl (painting@peggystodgill.com)
Wilson, Ann p47b, p49t, p62t, p66t, p72t, 80t (davanwilson@aol.com)

All other artwork belongs to Di Singleton.

Many thanks to Tru-Color Systems Inc (TCS) for the color conversion chart on p124.

While every effort has been made to credit contributors, Quarto would like to apologize should there have been any omissions or errors.

Dedication

I would like to dedicate this book to my lovely husband, John, without whose help and support, I couldn't have let painting take over my life. Uncomplaining, he follows me round craft fairs, helping me set up, puts together wood pieces and tolerates the frequent invasions of eager painting students into our home, he ignores the dust and the wood pieces which infiltrate every corner of the house, and encourages me in every new enterprise.

I would also like to thank all the friends and teachers I have met from all over the world through painting. I have learned so much from you all and realize I have so much more to learn.

Di Singleton